PENNY STOCKS

Beginner's Guide to Penny Stock Trading, Investing, and Making Money With Penny Stock Market Mastery

(Ultimate Guide With Strategies & Techniques for Beginners)

Ronald Morgan

Published by Kevin Dennis

Ronald Morgan

All Rights Reserved

Penny Stocks: Beginner's Guide to Penny Stock Trading, Investing, and Making Money With Penny Stock Market Mastery (Ultimate Guide With Strategies & Techniques for Beginners)

ISBN 978-1-989965-66-5

All rights reserved. No part of this guide may be reproduced in any form without permission in writing from the publisher except in the case of brief quotations embodied in critical articles or reviews.

Legal & Disclaimer

The information contained in this book is not designed to replace or take the place of any form of medicine or professional medical advice. The information in this book has been provided for educational and entertainment purposes only.

The information contained in this book has been compiled from sources deemed reliable, and it is accurate to the best of the Author's knowledge; however, the Author cannot guarantee its accuracy and validity and cannot be held liable for any errors or omissions. Changes are periodically made to this book. You must consult your doctor or get professional medical advice before using any of the suggested remedies, techniques, or information in this book.

Upon using the information contained in this book, you agree to hold harmless the Author from and against any damages, costs, and expenses, including any legal fees potentially resulting from the application of any of the information provided by this guide. This disclaimer applies to any damages or injury caused by the use and application, whether directly or indirectly, of any advice or information presented, whether for breach of contract, tort, negligence, personal injury, criminal intent, or under any other cause of action.

You agree to accept all risks of using the information presented inside this book. You need to consult a professional medical practitioner in order to ensure you are both able and healthy enough to participate in this program.

Table of Contents

INTRODUCTION 1

CHAPTER 1: AN INTRODUCTION TO PENNY STOCKS AND INVESTING 3

CHAPTER 2: WHAT ARE PENNY STOCKS? 28

CHAPTER 3: GETTING INTO THE TRADE 46

CHAPTER 4: CERTAIN THINGS ABOUT STOCKS EVERY TRADER NEEDS TO KNOW 62

CHAPTER 5: PENNY STOCK INVESTING 65

CHAPTER 6: PENNY STOCKS: AN OVERVIEW 76

CHAPTER 7: HOW TO START? 87

CHAPTER 8: A QUICK PENNY STOCKS VOCABULARY LESSON 90

CHAPTER 9: WHAT ARE PENNY STOCKS? 97

CHAPTER 10: NEGATIVE SITUATIONS 104

CHAPTER 11: SUCCESSFUL STOCK TRADERS HAVE STUDY HABITS. 116

CHAPTER 12: GETTING STARTED WITH PENNY STOCKS . 120

CHAPTER 13: PINK SHEET TRADING AND ITS PROFITABILITY 129

CHAPTER 14: IDENTIFYING PENNY STOCK SCAMS 145

CHAPTER 15: SOME TECHNIQUES & STRATEGIES 152

CHAPTER 16: PENNY STOCK DAY TRADING 162

CHAPTER 17: MISTAKES TO AVOID 168

CHAPTER 18: METHODS USED TO PREDICT TRADING 177

CHAPTER 19: THE DIFFERENCE IN PENNY STOCK TRADING. IN THE US, CANADA AND UK. 183

CHAPTER 20: THE SECRETS TO MAKING PROFIT 191

CHAPTER 21: TRADING PENNY STOCKS 197

CONCLUSION 205

Introduction

This book has actionable information on how to invest in penny stocks, trade penny stocks and make money in the process.

Investing in stocks is undoubtedly one of the best investment vehicles the world over. And it is not just the high value stocks that cost tens, hundreds or even thousands of dollars per share; even if you invest in stocks that cost less than $10 or even less than $5 per share, you stand a good chance to make a lot of money in the process, especially in capital gains. If you cannot afford to spare 10s, 100s or even 1000s of dollars per share, perhaps penny stocks are the way to go. Even if you are completely new to stocks trading and penny stocks in particular, you can learn everything there is to learn about these and succeed at it. There is just so much money to be made trading in penny stocks and this book will show you exactly what you need to do.

If you are one of those people who think that you have to be a trading prodigy to invest in penny stocks then you are very wrong. Penny stocks, just like any other stocks and securities, require you to be well informed, disciplined and have good strategies while participating in order to succeed- and this is what this guide is meant for. It will give you sufficient knowledge that you will require to get started as a penny stock trader inclusive of how to trade, calculating your profits, avoiding penny stocks hazards and much more!

This is where your penny stock success journey begins.

Chapter 1: An Introduction To Penny Stocks And Investing

A Note on Investing

As I was outlining where to start with penny stocks, I think it is important to first have a frank discussion about investing as a whole. If you are familiar with the ideas and mechanics behind investing, then this will be nothing new to you. Still, if you are unfamiliar with traditional stock exchanges or have had few major investments in companies over the last few years, it is worth doing a quick refresher. As such, the ideas in this section are applicable to both penny stock investments and traditional investments in companies located on traditional exchanges.

Every company wants capital for future investments. From Apple to McDonald's, all companies are looking towards the future. The future is going to be expensive for investment; this much is known. What that true cost will be is hidden behind inflation rates, what the company seeks to provide in the future, and increased governmental regulation on any sectors a company wishes to become involved with. To ensure that a company is in a suitable position to invest in the future, they need to raise capital. This capital is money that a company will eventually use to iterate on products in the future. The most common way of receiving a large sum of capital for a major company is to sell stock in a company. Even if you are familiar with these ideas, there are a couple of interesting mathematical principles in regards to how stocks, shares and market capitalization intersect.

Market capitalization is the total amount that a company is theoretically worth at a given time. For example, let's say that I create a company that specializes in making coffee. I create shares for my company to sell to investors, and suppose that there are 100 shares sold at $10 each. My total market capitalization based on these estimates is just $1000. Meaning, the total sum that I could possible use to invest in my company is $1000. This is a small scale example, but this is how the market capitalization of large companies is deduced as well. You take the number of outstanding shares of a company and multiply that by the current stock price, thus giving you the market capitalization. You can therefore start to see the connection between the number of shares a company has, the share price, and their capital positioning for future investment.

Based on the example above, the principles of market cap, a company has its best interest in ensuring that the stock price stays at a high value. Any drop in the stock price lowers the overall amount that a company can invest in future products. A drop in value makes it more difficult to take out a loan, which is usually measured against what the total market capitalization of a company is. With my coffee company for example, unless I provide additional evidence that my company will be a success, no bank would loan my coffee company $2000 when the market capitalization of that company simply isn't that large.

Everything in this section is a very simplified view on investments, but I want you to take away three very specific points. One, there is a relationship between the total outstanding shares, the price per share and the market capitalization of a company. Two, every company is interested in seeking financial backing to better position themselves for the future. Three, companies need to be looking towards future growth to have a good evaluation for today's stock price, meaning a company needs to be forward thinking to keep it's stock price high. You would never want to invest in a company that wasn't planning on improving their efficiency and product, even if that company is currently doing very well. These are the three basic principles of what companies are looking for when they are seeking investment. It is these three ideas that you will be tying yourself into, making decisions of where to invest that benefit you as much as possible, while having minimal concern about the health and benefit of the company that you invested in. There are exceptions for how long you will stay invested in a company, but in general you want to gain profit and cash out quickly.

What Are Penny Stocks?

For every large well known brand name company, there are at least ten smaller companies trying to offer the same service or product. If traditional stock exchanges serve the largest of these companies, it is then penny stocks that serve the smaller companies. Penny stocks are investment opportunities in small companies, companies that are not well known and are not listed on traditional stock exchanges. Penny stocks are often startups, but their size and product line can surprise even seasoned investors. The one universal truth that links all companies that sell penny stock is that they are all underleveraged and are all seeking outside investment.

It is very easy for a large company to raise money, and ironically, they are often the ones that need the least outside investment. If Microsoft wanted to create a new product that was financial intensive, they would have two options. They could either use there own reserves of wealth to finance the project, or they could seek outside investment and pay returns to investors, provided the product is a success. For Microsoft, the option is clear, they will take the outside investment money because it is less dangerous that betting on a new product with their already realized profits. Their incentive to do this is that they are creating a new product with the financial backing of the public based on the perception of the value of Microsoft as a whole. I understand that this is where financial investing can get a little complicated, but the basic premise is that there is less risk to Microsoft if they seek outside investment in the form of selling shares versus opening their own coffers to creating a new product.

The fundamental difference between a large company like Microsoft and the average company selling penny stocks is that the smaller company is starving financially. These are new companies that often have not released a product yet. They do not have the reserves to continue research and development. Even if they have completed their product through outside investment, they likely still need additional resources to market, manufacture and sell their product. With few large financial firms willing to back these small companies, it is then up to penny stock share holders to finance small firms.

This is where you and I come in; we search through the companies currently seeking investment, and purchase shares in promising companies. We receive the **opportunity** to become invested in these small companies because larger financial firms are simply too large to notice such small and budding companies. Often it is not an issue of investment, or rather the money required to lift one of these penny stock companies off the ground. It is simply that large financial firms are so large that small companies are not worth their time. They can seek returns just fine by investing in larger companies, something that investors like you and I cannot do.

It is difficult for small time investors like us to get involved in larger exchanges with bigger companies because large financial firms have this market on total lockdown. Between the high capital requirements and high frequency trading machines (more in this in a moment), smaller investors have much more room for profitability by investing in penny stocks. The size of the companies for investment match perfectly for what we are able to offer in terms of actual investment dollars. There are many ways to make money off of penny stocks, including not actually having a concern about what a penny stock company is producing, however the basic premise is still a small company that is seeking outside investment and cannot be listed on large, well known, public stock exchange.

Why Do Companies Choose Be listed as a Penny Stock?

It's important to note exactly **why** companies choose to be listed on penny stock exchanges. Remember that what these companies are seeking is merely outside investment. There are two major ways of seeking such investment, pubic and private. On the public side, a company that is listed as a penny stock investment typically did not meet the requirements to be listed on traditional stock exchanges like the NASDAQ or Dow Jones Industrial. These exchanges only take the largest companies, and even then it is quite difficult to get an official listing. Proof of this can be found all over, with the most recent example coming from a biomedical company that recently purchased

Majesco. Majesco for years worked in the entertainment and software industry, typically publishing small educational titles in Europe. The biomedical company that purchased, or more correctly was purchased by, Majesco is something called a 'buy in'. That is when a larger company merges with a smaller company not to receive any assets other than the name and corporate structure of the company that it is merging into. The biomedical company wanted to purchase Majesco purely because they were already listed on a large stock exchange. This is proof of how difficult it can be to get listed, even when you have a stable company with steady profits coming in. It was easier for this biomedical company to simply purchase an established name, albeit from a failing company, and then merge to take offer the ticker symbol. This is a traditional form of public investment, and type that you are most familiar with. As you can see, this first avenue of public investment is prohibitively expensive for most companies that are listed as penny stocks.

The second type of investment that a company can receive is private. This typically happens by a small company going around to different venture capital firms, as well as smaller private investors, and seeking capital directly to further the company. It is almost a certainty that most companies eventually listed as penny stocks started by seeking outside investment. This could have come in the form of familial help, or investment by the partners of the company itself. The reasons that other larger firms would have turned down this small companies are numerous. For a venture capital firm to make an investment in a company on the scale that I am describing is not an inexpensive venture. One firm would be taking on a brunt of the total investment capital required for a small company. It means that they only invest in what they believe have the highest chances for success. In addition, if a company is competing in a market where a different company that they have already invested in exists, you can almost certainly bet that a venture capital firm will pass on investment. It goes against their interest to have two competing companies, if each individual company requires multiple hundreds of thousands of dollars, or more.

For small companies then, you can see traditional public investment is ruled out, as well as private investment. There is yet one option left for small companies; to be listed as a penny stock. This allows for a small scale type of public investment. They do not need to fill out the extensive paperwork and go through all of the requirements of being listed on a large exchange, and they also do not need to gain multiple thousands of dollars from any single investor. What these companies get is the best of both worlds – they are able to seek investment from many different investors, and are not beholden to any single investor for such a large sum of money that they w0uold have to change the business model or product line. In essence, while being listed as a penny stock has distinct advantages for a small company, in the end it ultimately comes down to practicality. It is simply the best case for a company to be listed on a small public exchange as this is their best chance of gaining financial backing.

Advantages of Penny Stocks

As a beginner investor getting your feet wet with penny stocks, you have two primary advantages in trading in this market over more traditional stock exchanges. One, the capital requirements for penny stocks are incredibly low, and with jumps in stock price that are many magnitudes greater than traditional exchanges, profits can more easily be realized for smaller investors. Two, investors can trade with their best intentions, relying on their wit and research to find profitable companies. They can do this because they do not have the interference of high frequency trading algorithms.

The first major advantage is quite simple. Penny stocks got their namesake for the very reason that you might assume; they are often traded at or below one dollar. While there are exceptions to this one dollar clause (the Securities and Exchange Commission defines penny stocks as trading at under five dollars), the point still remains that penny stocks are inexpensive. What this means is that an investor can buy multiple shares of several different companies for the same cost that they would be able to buy a handful of shares of a single company on a major exchange. This allows for more diverse investment, and opens up strategies for diversification that is simply not available to undercapitalized traders working on traditional stock exchanges. Like with traditional stocks, a lot of the profitability in penny stocks is made from the small jumps in a stock's price. The jumps and percentage change found in penny stocks is completely unrivaled. It means that for even day traders, a specialized type of trading that I'll go into more detail in chapter three, there is lots of profitability to be made over the few hours between market open and market close. They can make diversified bets across multiple companies due to the low cost of entry, and cash out making profit at the end of the day because the types of changes due to volatility is quite large. The low cost of entry is our starting point to penny stocks, and opens the door for our tier of investment, but it is hardly the biggest thing that penny stocks have going for them.

It is my opinion that high frequency trading has all but ruined traditional markets for the small to medium tier investor. You might be familiar with high frequency trading, as in recent years it has received some coverage, yet I'm all too shocked by the number of early investors that are completely unaware of this phenomenon. It is by and far the largest reason why I turned away from traditional exchanges to focus on penny stocks. A high frequency trading operation functions by having a computer buy and sell stock at a rate of hundreds of trades every fraction of a second. The stock that a computer purchases is often only held for a minutes. You can probably already start to see the large scale damage high frequency trading can have on regular investors. No matter how fast you are, you'll never be as fast as a computer. This issue with speed comes in two forms. The first is that these computers can simply think must faster humans. The calculations that a high frequency trading computer runs are so complex, but done instantaneously. These operations function due to complex algorithms, or formulas for what stock to buy and in what amounts. The computer that purchases stock does not care about the underlying value, or the product that a company is selling. It simply has a profile that if X company drops below Y value, purchase Z company if trading below T price – high frequency trading computers are built around these strings of logic, but are often so complex that it would take months dissecting the code to understand the logic of stock purchases. To illustrate the complexity and unknowns, one must only look to recent history. Not too long ago the Dow Jones lost five hundred points in a matter of hours, and then saw a recovery later in that day. This rapid fluctuation had investors worried, and it was only later discovered that due to a series of high frequency trading computers competing against each other, that they started a rapid sell off that resulted in the Dow dropping hundreds of points very quickly. Not only are these computers thinking much faster than investors, they are working on a set of logic that humans simply do not operate. They are looking only at the value of stock, and are holding stock based on the premise that they can unload stock faster than anyone else, which they can.

The second issue with high frequency trading and their lighting fast trades is the proximity these computers have to the central servers that handle trades for major exchanges. Not too long ago, the New York real estate market in midtown Manhattan became muddled due to large firms seeking to buy land as close as possible to the New York Stock Exchange (NYSE). Their reason for wanting to buy land close to the exchange was to place their high frequency trading computers as close as possible to the NYSE's central servers. These machines are so fast that eventually the limiting factor in terms of making successful trades was based on the proximity a computer had to the central server. Suddenly being 200 miles away from the server was too far, as competing machines did better the closer they got to the central exchange. Today, the NYSE actually rents space out themselves for investors, so that high frequency trading machines can compete on a level playing field. While that is all good and fine for these trading machines, it just goes to further illustrate the point that small to medium sized investors have become less and less competitive on traditional markets. It is a huge benefit then to penny stock investors that we do not have to deal with such high frequency trading machines, and likely never will. While some investors have tried to create machines for penny stocks, the number of companies and the type of information that these machines trade on is simply not conducive to this type of algorithmic trading. In penny stocks, it is human intellect that reigns supreme.

Disadvantages of Penny Stocks

As you learn more about penny stocks and the strategies to realizing profit, you will begin to learn to see the limitations. You will need my advice to stave off the potential trouble spots of investing in penny stocks, of which there are numerous. Don't let anything in this section alarm you, as even what can seem like a negative to penny stocks can actually be used to realize profit. That being said, there are real negatives that exist to trading in penny stocks; investors open themselves up to corporate fraud, a company suddenly going under and outside manipulation of the market.

Corporate fraud is probably the most common trouble spot when it comes to penny stocks. To be listed on a large exchange requires months of auditing, to ensure that financial documents are up to date and accurate. While the financial documents of many smaller companies are not nearly as complicated as any company listed on the NADSAQ, it opens up new challenges. Penny stocks are poorly regulated on a company by company basis. That is, the market as a whole has a decent set of regulations in place, but inspecting any one company is so time intensive that it just isn't done as well as on the larger exchanges. What ends up happening is that companies will lie on financial reports. These can be minor changes, but the impact can be quite brutal. These companies are simply trying to raise their stock price and get more investment capital to finalize and ship their product. Many managers and CEOs of these small companies will list inaccurate statements on financial forms because they believe in the product that is being made. They feel that the ends justify the means; the problem is that in one way or another, when corporate fraud becomes apparent, it is the investors that are left holding the short end of the stick. There are strategies to avoid getting caught up in losing money from this type of corporate fraud, but it is worth noting that it is particularly endemic to penny stock trading and is not nearly as prevalent with companies on larger exchanges.

The second major issue with companies listed on penny stock exchanges is that they can disappear overnight. Since increased regulation in the mid 2000s, this has been less of a problem, but it is still a regular occurrence. If you do not research a company heavily enough, or do not pay attention to the history of its stock price, you leave yourself open to possibly to possibly falling prey to investing at exactly the wrong time. It's quite easy to avoid falling into this trap, but it can still happen to the best of us. Whereas on traditional exchanges you may see the price of a stock decline significantly, chances are your total investment in that company is never completely wiped out. With companies that sell penny stock, the odds of a company going completely under and becoming unlisted is much higher. In this circumstance, every investment dollar in that company is completely wiped out, with none of it being recoverable at any time.

The third issue with penny stocks is that they are ripe for outside manipulation. Since penny stocks are not well known companies that typically have a large number of shares to sell at a very low price per share, it is quite easy for a public face to draw attention to a penny stock and see that price skyrocket. This is called a 'pump and dump' scheme. Essentially, a public figure purchases large quantities of a penny stock, makes a public statement about the company, usually to get investors excited about buying in. Investors then flock to this company, driving the stock price up and then the public facing figure sells all of their stock. They profit from the great change in price between when they bought the stock and sold it after selling the name to the public. Occurrences of this have declined massively in the last ten years, but it is always a risk. At the same time, the last time something like this happened, I actually made quite a bit profit. As with all of the negatives I have listed in this section, there are ways to either bypass the difficulty brought on from these negative attributes of penny stocks, or there are ways to actually earn profit from some of these issues arising.

The Winning Secret of Penny Stocks

I am going to teach you many ways of getting ahead and gaining profit through penny stocks. That being said, there is one strategy that is difficult to pull off, but should success find an investor, he or she can make become extremely wealthy in a short period of time. I'm referring to a penny stock company breaking through into the mainstream. Remember that you are getting in on the ground floor of many of these companies. You are getting in a time when there is little investment and so for each dollar you invest, you are earning a sizable chunk of that company's total backing. Think about the smaller investors in Facebook or Google, investors that sewed up a few thousands dollars in a small company for a fraction of a percentage ownership of the brand. These small investments grew to be worth many multiple millions of dollars due to the company breaking through and proving to be a mainstream success. While the odds of striking another Google or Facebook are low, it is a possibly that exists in penny stocks that is completely absent from major exchanges. Companies that are listed on large exchanges have already had their breakthrough moment, and the best an investor can hope for is steady growth into the future. For penny stock investors, there will be dozens of companies that fail, but if one can realize even moderate success, the profitability to the investor can easily be in the hundreds of thousands of dollars.

Chapter 2: What Are Penny Stocks?

Welcome to the wonderful and often stressful world of Penny Stocks. Your investment future is of vital importance and beginning your financial future by investing in Penny Stocks will do more than just earn you return on investment, it will educate you on the world of stocks, trades, and portfolio investments. Before you dive into Penny Stocks, however, you first need to understand what they are. In the following Chapter we will discuss what penny stocks are, their history, how they compare to higher priced stocks, the basic who, what, where, when, and why's, and a thorough explanation of the broker/representative/financial advisor relationship and how it can help and hurt you in your investment future. Everything in this chapter is meant to give you a platform base to start from, and you never want to jump into any investment without knowing exactly what it is and how it will work for you.

The actual definition of Penny Stocks has evolved throughout the years. Originally it was defined as any stock that is traded for under a dollar per share. However, the SEC has since changed that definition to include any stock that is sold for under five dollars a share, broadening your choices when working with Penny Stocks. Most of the companies that you will find that are categorized as Penny Stocks do not trade on the major market exchanges, with a few exceptions. The companies you will be looking into for trading purposes will be small businesses with high liquidity and are subject to limited listing with fewer regulatory requirements. These stocks are often very high risk because these companies are often growing and have limited resources. However, with greater risk can come higher return on investment so don't let the fact that most Penny Stocks are high risk deter you from this type of investment.

History

Penny stocks can be used interchangeably with the term micro-cap stocks. Micro-cap stocks are technically considered as such because of the market capitalizations they are capable of, while Penny stocks are considered on the basis of their price. In general, a stock with a capitalization of fifty dollars and three hundred million dollars is a micro cap. Definitions often vary when it comes to penny stocks because while the Securities and Exchange Commission lists penny stocks as any under five dollars, some set the cut-off point at three dollars and others only consider stocks under one dollar penny stocks. Primarily, however, any stock on the pink sheet or over-the-counter bulletin board to be a penny stock. Since definitions change from place to place, it is important to research with your point of purchase what they consider to be penny stocks. Most of the time, however, if you are signing up to trade penny stocks, that is the only type of stock you will be presented with.

What Makes Penny Stocks So High Risk?

We will get into the difference between levels of risk later on in this book, but to explain penny stocks better, it is important to understand the good and the bad. By definition, high risk investments are those that carry a strong chance that you could lose some or all of your investment. Now don't let that immediately scare you away, the opposite and the biggest reason so many people choose high-risk investments is because your rate of return is often exponentially larger than other types of risk investments. Penny stocks fall into the high-risk category for four reasons which are the lack of substantial information available, the fact that there are little to no minimum standards for the company to follow, penny stocks usually belong to new businesses, so there is little background information available, and their liquidity. Let's dive a little bit further into these four factors that make penny stock high risk.

Lack Of Solid Information Available

One of the biggest parts of forming a successful portfolio is having sufficient information to make educated choices on your investments. For penny stocks, information on the company is often tough to find. A company that is listed on pink sheets face subtle requirements and do not have to file with the SEC and therefore are not publicly scrutinized and regulated as the larger stocks that appear on the New York Stock Exchange and the Nasdaq. Often the information that you do find is not produced from credible sources. When you are investing in penny stocks, always research the root from where your information is coming from, and if it is a paid advertiser or broker, then you may want to look into other avenues. Most companies that are traded are available for contact as well so feel free to reach out to them directly, though their information will be inherent bias.

Very Little Background Information Available

It is often discovered that many of the penny stock or micro-cap stocks have either just formed as a company or are nearing bankruptcy. When a company is brand new there is inherently no background information for them to give so you will have little to go off of. When a corporation is nearing bankruptcy, they either have not done a good job keeping historical records or they keep them from the public view. If you are researching a company and have found they have been in business for a while but have little background information you should probably move on to a different company. Remember that not all penny stock companies fall into one of these categories, but it is best to understand the worse case scenario before you start investing money into these unknown businesses. It is very rare that you will find a well-known company in the penny stock arena, so research is essential in this line of investments.

Lack Of Minimum Standards

Standard requirements are way less stringent for stocks on the OTCBB and pink sheets and therefore are less likely to be monitored closely. There is also a chance that this is exactly why a stock is on one of those exchanges. A lot of times when a company is no longer able to meet the requirements of the major exchanges they join the pink sheets or the OTCBB. The OTCBB is slightly more stringent with their rules and requires companies to file their paperwork in a strict timeframe with the SEC. The pink sheets have no such requirement and can often be a haven for businesses that want to stay under the radar but still on the market. The minimum standards we are talking about can be considered a safety net for investors and a goal or bragging right for the company. Knowing your investment in stock is protected by at least the minimum standards a company should adhere to can help you feel more comfortable when investing your money.

Liquidity

Liquidity in the stock market is defined as the amount of action the stock is receiving during a particular period. When a stock doesn't have a high liquidity in can become tough to sell that stock. If the level of liquidity is considered small, you may be able to find a buyer, but you will most likely be required to lower the price of the stock in order to attract those customers. A low liquidity can also lend to fraud or manipulation of the share prices. The easiest way to manipulate these stocks is by buying massive amounts of stock, get people excited about it, and then sell it after other investors start to become interested. This manipulation is usually done by the company or by someone very familiar with the stock industry and is known as pump and dump in the investment world. Make sure always to do your due diligence when it comes to investments and don't listen to the hype by random investors or companies.

Common Scams To Watch Out For

With the minimum standards that penny stock companies need to reach and the lack of knowledge and background information on these businesses, penny stocks can fall victim to scams pretty quickly. The SEC regards these types of stocks a pain in their butts, but they continue to allow the investment community to take part since it can be incredibly lucrative when done the correct way. There are many different scams out there, but the two most used are the recommendations based on biased backgrounds and the brokers offshore. Again, these are not anywhere near the only two scams that are circulating the penny stock industry, but these are definitely two of the most famous and the most important for you to be aware of. Let's take a closer look at both types of scams and how to avoid them.

Biased Recommendations

There are some companies out there that will pay people or businesses to recommend their stock to you. These recommendations will come in many different ways including newsletters, radio, and commercial television. Even your email will not be safe from this biased salesman and you could receive spam that is attempting to entice you into purchasing specific stocks. You should never take any of these false promotions seriously, and you should also stay away from those particular investments. A dead giveaway that you are being made victim to this scam is a disclaimer providing the information that the advertiser is being paid by someone to represent this investment stock. Press releases are also ways that these stocks can be promoted, so you want to make sure you find out the legitimacy of any press release you read before taking its advice and purchasing the stock.

Brokers Offshore

Regulations by the SEC allow companies to sell stock outside of the United States to investors and are exempt from registering that stock. Companies will sell the stock to foreign brokers at a discounted rate. The brokers then, after purchasing the stock, turn around and sell it back to U.S. investors for a huge profit. These agents use high-pressure tactics to sell this stock such as cold calling investors that have substantial financial availability to purchase the stock and give misleading but attractive information about the assets in order to get the investors to buy the stock. These brokers also employ very harsh sales tactics when attempting to sell their shares which are not the typical action of an investment broker. To be safe stay away from all foreign agents and choose to work with brokers that work for reputable and well-known firms if you decide to go that route. Anyone cold-calling for investments is not usually someone you want to trust with your financial future.

Broker/Financial Planner Relationship

When you are entering the financial investment arena, you will be faced with the decision to employ an investment broker and/or a financial advisor. These two people do different things but can be useful in specific situations. All in all, however, penny stocks are not really the types of investments you will want to employ a broker or advisor for since their cost could quickly eat up your profit. Regardless of that, it is vital for you to understand both of these positions and how they can work for you as you continue to diversify your portfolio and possibly enter into the larger stock arena. Advisors can also be useful resources when attempting to do research on specific stocks or investments. We are going to take a look at both the investment broker and the financial advisor and the duties of both of them.

Broker

An investment broker is a person that brings companies selling stock together with an investor looking to purchase stock. Investment brokers are usually required to be licensed and can work for both the seller and the buyer in the stock management arena. Generally, the agent only acts on behalf of the client and follows their instructions. Agents are paid through fees charged for services which can range in price depending on the firm, the job, and the stock that is being worked with. Three of the main ways that brokers make their money is through commissions, margin interest charges, and fees for service. Beyond handling the stocks for clients, brokers are often also allowed to provide investment advice and offer limited banking services such as check writing and opening interest bearing savings accounts, but they primarily work strictly with selling and buying stocks for their clients. The main thing you need to know is that you will sometimes have to work with brokers and when it is not demanded you need to know when it will be helpful.

Brokers aren't going to give you the ins and outs of increasing your portfolio and their service fees for investment advice can sometimes be absolutely astronomical. You want to remember that, though we hope the people handling our money have integrity, brokers work for both the company and the investor so taking investment advice can sometimes be biased. When you really need to decide on hiring or using brokerage services is when you are planning to purchase larger or restricted stocks in the major markets. Some of the stocks on the main markets are required to use a broker to go between the company and the investor and are not publicly sold. You can get a broker by using the brokers at the company in which you trade through, or you can hire a broker from a local firm. The brokers working for the larger financial firms usually have their finger on the pulse of the investment world and often charge way less of a fee than hiring someone privately to handle your purchases. Either way, brokers are not necessary for penny stocks nor do many of them offer their services in that field.

Financial Advisor

Technically financial advisors can be considered brokers, lawyers, planners, etc. so for this book we are going to talk about planners. Financial planners are professionals that assist their clients in setting up a plan for their financial investments and portfolios. You can find financial planners at firms and also through your bank. The charges that you may incur from a financial planner depend on your level of services and what financial investments you choose to participate in through this professional. The important part of a planner is to get you into a financial position to engage in the investment world and create a diversified portfolio. Most investments made through a financial planner are your lower risk investments such as IRA's, bonds, and high-interest bank accounts. Most financial planners are not brokers, but many brokers are also financial planners though their loyalties are often in conflict due to their buyer/seller relationships.

Financial planning can be extremely expensive, but there comes the point in almost every person's financial investment plan that a planner is necessary. One superb reason to hire a planner would be when you reach a period in your financial future that you are unsure of what the next step should be. When you hit these walls with your financial investment future, it is important to hire someone that can lead you in the right direction. Another good reason to hire a professional is when you look at money and financial planning, and you just have no interest in handling it yourself. These moments can easily lead to no or little planning which can be detrimental to your financial future so make sure to go to the professional if this is just not your cup of tea. Also, if you are taking a self-promote position in handling your own finances, you may want to hire a planner in order to be an impartial person to review your plan. By using a planner for a review, you are assuring yourself the best plan possible since they will be able to offer better or more lucrative solutions to your investment and portfolio project.

Whether you are looking to bring a professional into your project or just looking to the future, the information in this chapter has given you a solid understanding of the investment world. Penny stocks may have risks and may not be something you want to sink all of your money into, but they can result in very lucrative investment returns if you choose to follow the guidelines and safety rules that we have expressed so far in this book. Making financial choices is paramount but can be very nerve racking without the proper education. Creating a diverse portfolio is imperative to reaching your financial goals for the future and penny stocks are definitely an amazing way to give your portfolio that diversification. Penny stocks are also great learning tools for when you decide to move into larger more expensive stocks but remember that they are way less restrictive and usually a bit higher risk than those stocks on the major exchanges. Do your research, decide intelligently on assistance through brokers and planners, and you have no choice but to be successful in your endeavors with penny stocks and micro-cap investments. Now that you understand penny stocks it is now time to begin preparing for your investment future.

Chapter 3: Getting Into The Trade

Since you discover more about working with Penny Stocks, the time has come to take a shot at placing some cash into the Stocks that you might want to utilize and ensuring that you get the correct Stocks that will assist you with bringing in the cash that you might want from this kind of venture. This part is going to assist you with figuring out how to begin with Penny Stocks so you can see the benefits that you need in the blink of an eye.

Opening Your Account

The absolute initial step for you to do when beginning on Penny Stocks is to open an exchanging account. As a financial specialist, you have to consider how simple it is for the record arrangement, the client assistance with the record, and any expenses that are related with opening and running the record. There are times when a representative will pick a fixed rate for a littler measure of offers however this rate can increment when you exchange on more offers; contingent upon the kind of exchanging that you do, this could have a major effect in the benefit that you make.

The beneficial thing about taking a shot at a commission for each offer thought is that it functions admirably for financial specialists who need to get into Penny Stocks however who don't have a great deal of additional cash for it. As a speculator, you should search around so as to locate the best representatives and the best exchanging accounts request to expand your benefits so set aside the effort to glance around and converse with a couple of various merchants to figure out which one is the best for you to get into.

Picking Your Penny Stocks

At the point when you are prepared to discover a Penny Stock and settle on a choice, you should browse either the Over-the-Counter Bulletin Board or from the Pink Sheets. You will discover a rundown of Stocks that are accessible for you to buy and you can do your examination and pick the correct ones. A few representatives will give you some screening devices so you are better as far as picking the Stocks in accordance with your hazard resistance level and your contributing technique.

Since Penny Stocks are an extremely unpredictable speculation, it is conceivable to rake in boatloads of cash from your venture, however it is additionally altogether conceivable to lose a ton of cash in the process too.

There aren't many individuals who put resources into Penny Stocks, a portion of the market players incorporate cash chiefs, file reserves, and different shared assets, which is one reason why Penny Stock market is so unstable. Since there aren't that numerous speculators that go with this alternative, you may encounter liquidity issues now and again. You will be unable to sell a portion of the Stocks that you own in light of the fact that there sufficiently aren't purchasers accessible who might take your Stock by any stretch of the imagination, substantially less at the value that you might want. You may need to assume a major misfortune and sell them at a much lower value you might want. Yet, there is additionally a likelihood that these Stocks will go the other way and you can sell them at an a lot higher incentive than you bought them. Yet, it is the activity of the financial specialist to choose what direction this will go before making an acquisition of a Penny Stock.

Choosing a Broker

An intermediary is a notable individual who will assist you with beginning on Penny Stocks. A specialist will be responsible for giving you the stage that you need so as to chip away at your exchanges. They can work with you to give a few proposals to what Stocks to buy, just as giving advertising and deals administrations to all partners. They will have a ton of apparatuses and exhortation that you will require when you begin. Each merchant that you work with will have various administrations and apparatuses that you can use, so this ought to go into thought with regards to selecting the representatives you need to work with.

A significant number of the intermediaries you need to consider will have a decent nearness on the web and some of them will offer exchanging stages that deal with cell phones. You can likewise work with some that offer ledgers for exchanging these offers. Regardless of what technique you are utilizing for your exchanging and which one you believe is ideal, it is significant that you pick a merchant who can give you dependable and moment cash moves so you can finish your exchanges at the perfect time.

On the off chance that your agent is delayed at executing any requests you put, you may wind up missing out on a great deal of cash since you pay more than anticipated for the Stock or they aren't brisk enough at getting you out of the game, so be cautious with this when working with them.

Some different things that you ought to consider while picking a stock intermediary are the expenses and charges they are offering to you. All specialists need a few expenses to assist them with playing out their activity, yet gain directly from the earliest starting point the amount they are going to charge you and what everything relies upon, (for example, on the off chance that they charge one rate for a modest quantity of exchanges and, at that point another rate for resulting exchanges, and so on.). Continuously take a gander at the terms and conditions on the site of your dealers and see with your own eyes in the event that you can concur with everything expressed there.

Rules to Ensure You Make a Profit When Trading Penny Stocks

While there will be some hazard when you get into Penny Stocks, there are a couple of decides that you have to follow to make it simpler so as to bring in some cash with Penny Stocks. Probably the most well-known principles that are best for your exchanging include:

1. The speculator needs to have an arrangement set up directly from the beginning that encourages them to know their entering and leaving procedure. This assists with keeping a portion of the feelings out of the game.

2. The speculator has to know when the time has come to exit. You should cut your misfortunes when the market begins to turn out to be more flighty with the goal that you don't lose more cash than you need to.

3. The speculator needs to ensure that the prize is bigger than the hazard. You never ought to go into an exchange that appears as a definite misfortune.

4. The speculator must have a decent plan for dealing with their cash. They should consistently remember this while picking a Penny Stock.

5. The speculator ought to never exchange utilizing their feelings. This is an assurance approach to prompt a major misfortune that will deteriorate when feelings become possibly the most important factor.

6. The speculator ought to abstain from exchanging during the primary hour of the day. There are numerous more seasoned speculators who utilize this chance to take a shot at offering offers to learners and they realize that the cost will go down. They want to make a benefit during this time before the Stock goes down. Along these lines, hold up a couple of hours and afterward do your exchanging.

7. The speculator ought to never put away more cash than they can lose. It is conceivable to procure a decent benefit on the off chance that you are brilliant about your speculations yet never get so into the game that you contribute more than you need to lose.

Learning to Minimize Your Risks

With regards to Penny Stocks, understand this is a hazardous venture. You are not working with a typical stock that are on the standard Stock Exchange, consequently getting the necessary data that you need so as to settle on flawless choices is practically unthinkable. While you can rake in tons of cash with Penny Stocks, it is additionally conceivable to lose a great deal of cash simultaneously.

Fortunately, there are sure things that you can do so as to seriously limit your hazard with Penny Stocks. There are a couple of things that you should keep an eye out for in light of the fact that these assistance to show which Penny Stock is too hazardous to even consider working with. For instance, in the event that you notice that an organization has a little activity and just an unassuming business sector capitalization, it is one of the more dangerous speculations. Something else to look out for is Stocks that sell excessively low.

A few people feel that all huge organizations began with Penny Stocks and this is the reason they decide to go into this sort of speculation. There are a not many that do begin as Penny Stocks to get the assets that they need before moving into the Stock market, however this is strange and most organizations don't work along these lines.

So for what reason are a few organizations keen on offering Penny Stocks when there are different choices? A few organizations will go with Penny Stock when they need to pay for something costly in the organization or when they are hoping to grow. The organization can offer Penny Stocks so as to disseminate a portion of its benefits and make changes to its assessment structure every year. Some financier firms will persuade organizations to present these Stocks on the grounds that the specialists need to procure cash from speculators. A few organizations will considerably offer Penny Stocks on the off chance that it discovers that they won't develop any longer later on and they might want to put the proprietorship on the speculators.

This is the reason you should be cautious about the Penny Stocks that you get into. Some are simply searching for some assistance to extend and they will be trustworthy choices that you can bring in some cash on in the event that you are cautious and do your exploration. Be that as it may, others are simply attempting to offload a portion of their obligations or they need to get a tax cut, instead of help you out, and you could wind up losing a ton of cash. At the point when you go into Penny Stocks, a decent method to consider it is that these organizations don't generally think about the speculators. In the event that you have this vigilant idea in your mind when contributing, you are bound to pick a Stock that benefits you the most, in the long haul.

Scams and Penny Stocks

Tricks are truly predominant inside the Penny Stocks world since they are not part of the typical Stock Exchange. A large number of the organizations don't keep the SEC principles so getting data that you need can be troublesome. It is simple for tricks to emerge in such circumstance.

As a speculator, you should be cautious with your cash and watch out for these tricks. There are numerous acceptable organizations you can exchange with and take in substantial income on, however there are additionally loads of awful intermediaries who will attempt to simply take your cash, awful organizations that need to bring in cash rapidly, and significantly different speculators who will fire raising their own Stocks and gain higher than they paid for a terrible Stock. You should be autonomous and figure out how to think all alone so you can get the best rate of profitability and not get taken in by one of the tricks.

Beginning on Penny Stocks is entirely simple as long as you realize which organizations to trust, choose a decent exchanging record, and locate a dealer who won't charge you a lot to work with. Include some great exploration and one of the exchanging procedures that we will discuss beneath, and you are good to go in bringing in some incredible cash with Penny Stocks.

Misconception About Penny Stocks

It is regular for individuals who need to bring in cash off these Penny Stocks to begin spreading a few bits of gossip and deception about how Penny Stocks will function. All things considered, you have heard eventually that numerous famous Stocks available today began as Penny Stocks. These gossipy tidbits are begun so as to get new financial specialists to buy Stocks that they wouldn't in any case at a more significant expense since they need to be in at a very early stage of an organization that will pull out all the stops. Nonetheless, as an industrious speculator, you will discover this isn't accurate at all and the main explanation that a portion of these organizations had Stocks that were worth less cash is on the grounds that they split up their Stocks, not on the grounds that they began as

Penny Stocks.

A few people likewise accept that on the grounds that an organization offers Penny Stocks, it isn't protected to exchange by any means. This is valid at times. There are a few organizations who simply need to bring in cash rapidly and afterward leave you with something that is useless, however there are additionally a few organizations that are utilizing this as an approach to get them out. The guidelines for jumping on the bigger Stock Exchange are entirely exacting and a few organizations are extremely extraordinary, however pass up a great opportunity by a smidgen for getting onto the regular Stock Exchange. They may begin as a Penny Stock while they chip away at making it to the primary Stock Exchange, hypothetically there is nothing in a general sense amiss with them. These are the organizations that you will need to wager on the grounds that they can make the best rate of profitability. It is never a smart thought to go into Penny Stocks believing that it is simple. There are numerous intermediaries and other people who are around here who will attempt to reveal to all of you their examples of overcoming adversity and attempt to persuade you that anybody can get into Penny Stocks and make a fortune. These individuals are typically attempting to get you to become tied up with something so they can get more cash-flow also.

There are a great deal of misguided judgments that are out there about Penny Stocks. Some of them might be valid, yet a significant number of them are a direct result of the buzz that is around the Penny Stocks to get you to buy them or they are from individuals who simply don't see how the market functions. Before you put away your well deserved cash, try to make a stride back and truly see how these sorts of Stocks work with the goal that you can settle on the most ideal choices.

Chapter 4: Certain Things About Stocks Every Trader Needs To Know

Before I unravel that great secret – this wonderful trick of making virtually certain profits – and place it in front of you, I want to tell you something real quickly. There are certain things about stocks every trader needs to know:

"Bulls Make Money, Bears Make Money, Pigs Get Slaughtered" –A popular Wall Street saying.

Warren Buffet (the greatest investor ever born, one who has made MORE MONEY in stocks than any other individual on the face of the earth) says that it's risky to expect more than 20 % returns per annum from stocks.

Why does Buffett say that? The answer is pretty straightforward: if we balance risks with rewards and opt for safer investments, it would be unwise to expect more than 20% price appreciation (yearly). Because if we go for higher profits we will end up compromising the safety of the investment and are likely to end up losing what we had rather than gaining what we wanted –exponential profits!

So the question here is, when stalwarts and masters like Buffett are cautioning us against making risky investments, is it prudent to invest in something as risky as a penny stock? After considering Warren Buffett's advice you must be wondering how can this writer (me) come up with a trading technique which can fetch a profit (often) in excess of 25% in matter of minutes(if not seconds!)–AND STILL MAY BE SAFE ENOUGH TO EMPLOY?

Guys, that's the beauty of this particular play :) The other great advantage in this play is that *unlike* Buffett, who (often) waits for years and years (after making an investment), to realize profit, one *doesn't* have to wait for eons to realize profit. Neither does one have to go the stock pundits and experts who advise/ recommend stocks promising all kinds of profits. Wonder why they need to be consultants for others when they can use their wisdom and expertise for their own profits? Anyway I am not here to analyze who does what. I am just sharing a way I discovered wherein there is a good opportunity of making quick and sizeable profit without taking unwarranted risk.

But before I share the technique and secret, I strongly encourage a new penny stock investor to study the following golden rules of trading (penny stocks) and take them to heart, before trading. (Please note that I keep stating "TRADING" and NOT INVESTING because Penny stocks are no instruments to invest in — they are there only good for trading—in n out!)

They have been contributed by some highly experienced traders on I-HUB.

Chapter 5: Penny Stock Investing

How Stock Investing Works

Many stock investing experts believe that penny stocks are worthless, that investing in small cap stocks is dangerous and that investors should avoid them at all costs. This view is valid in various respects, except that by completely ignoring penny stocks, you are throwing the baby out with the bath water. Applying yourself to analysing small cap stocks through identifying excellent small companies can reward you richly. You may discover a future giant. You see, the "enemies" of penny stocks do not take into account that gigantic companies whose shares are now all time "blue chips," once started as penny stocks.

When buying stocks you buy shares of a company. This company has decided to expand its activities, and to do that it needs money. One way of obtaining funds is to issue shares. The company has to be listed on the stock exchange, where the shares of all other listed companies are traded. Despite fluctuations, the share price of a prosperous company usually rises, but it can also drop when the company, for instance, does not show a profit. The price can also drop if the stock market as a whole has a downturn, often the result of broader economic problems, of a national or international nature. Sometimes a share gets a pounding because the sector of the market in which it operates suffers a drawback. Over time, however, the share prices of large, prosperous companies have risen dramatically, earning their shareowners huge fortunes. Today financial analysts show figures that confirm that stocks have outperformed all other investment instruments in the long term. Especially long-term investors are advised to keep a share portfolio in their investment portfolio to hedge them against inflation.

Selecting Good Stocks: Fundamental Analysis

As indicated above, you actually research the company and not the stock you are interested in. There are a number of guidelines to assist you when scrutinizing a company to determine whether it is worth investing in. The process is usually termed fundamental analysis. The greatest stock investor so far in history, Warren Buffett, uses only fundamental analysis to select stocks that meet his criteria.

We shall now discuss the criteria for selecting good stocks. Note that these criteria are applicable to all stocks. They entail Fundamental Analysis and Technical Analysis. After this, we turn to penny stocks to explain their specific characteristics and information on how to find them.

Four of the most important requirements when studying a company are:

• Product: Is the company's product something new, or does it fill a gap in a particular niche? Is it a quality product? If not a new product, will it compete effectively with existing products?

• Profitability: Does the company make a profit and has it made profits over a period of three or more years? What do its debt levels look like?

• Resilience: How robust is the company? Does it have the potential to withstand inflation, higher interest rates, a rise in fuel prices etc.?

• Management: Is the company's management competent? Are they people with integrity, good reputations and diligence? Do they publish financial reports regularly and on time? Do they have open communication with their shareholders? The CEO (Chief Executive Officer) plays a key role in the management of a company. Although this must be a consideration, it does not mean that a CEO with a magnificent record with one company will automatically achieve the same proficiency with another.

Selecting Good Stocks: Technical Analysis

Another method to uncover the best stocks to invest in is to use an instrument that is termed technical analysis. Technical analysis attempts to determine future price trends by analyzing factors such as previous prices, trade volumes etc. A variety of indicators presented as graphs show statistics on shares and market sectors. Using these indicators can give you an indication of the current achievements of market sectors, while also assisting you in selecting the best stocks in a specific sector. The most important value of technical analysis is that it assists you in your decision when to buy and when to sell a stock. Some of the most used technical indicators are moving averages, bar graphs, trend lines, support and resistance, volume, momentum, relative strength, overbought/oversold oscillators, and stock patterns such as head-and-shoulders formation. Since these indicators are presented as graphs, it will be necessary to consult internet websites that provide these technical graphs. To utilize technical indicators best, special stock market programs are available to assist you with technical analysis when you have become an advanced investor.

Penny Stocks

It is now time to take a closer look to arguments about penny stocks. To start with: what is a penny stock? Penny stocks (or penny shares) are similar to other shares that you buy on the stock market. The important difference is that penny shares are cheap to buy ($5 or less per share, but there is no consensus over the amount). Often new and small companies issue these shares with a much smaller market capitalization than other stocks. This explains why they are relatively cheap. Methods and techniques to select penny stocks do not differ radically from those used to pick other stocks.

Penny Stocks Versus Other Stocks

What do small cap (penny) stocks offer? Why are they a buying proposition for a small investor? There are quite a few answers. Firstly, not only are penny stocks affordable (and therefore within the reach of less affluent people), but there is more scope for their underlying companies to grow. The share price of a young, prosperous company that has proved itself over a period of more or less three years, often increases by 40%, 80%, 120% or even 400% within a short length of time. On the other hand, a so-called "blue chip" stock held by a large, established company and costing $45 per share, is unlikely to move with such leaps and bounds. Secondly, small cap stocks are often less prone to big market movements.

Admittedly there is another side to this argument as well. Let us be honest, the large majority of penny stocks are indeed worthless. One penny stock experts reckons that over 97% are complete failures. The reason for that is that the majority of small companies are duds, incapable of getting off the ground, resulting from inadequate financial resources, poor management or other problems. Therefore it is of utmost importance to find the pearls and to recognize the fly-by-night companies so that you can avoid them. In that sense it is true that penny stock investing is risky. By nature penny stocks are also more volatile than the more established stocks. However, the risk factor is not limited to penny stocks. The stocks of large companies can also be risky not only because they can fall victim to market crashes, but also when they perform poorly and prove to be a loss to big investors.

Bear in mind that the price of any share may drop as low as that of a penny share. In some cases even lower. The reasons for that do not necessarily differ from those causing the downturn of penny stocks. A number of reasons can be responsible for this, including losses made by the company, bad management or an extraordinary meltdown of a whole sector.

Where do I Find the Information?

The important point is that penny stock selection and trading do not exist in isolation. Small companies with huge growth potential and rock bottom stock prices may be identified in similar fashion than other stocks, but with more circumspection. That means you should acquire knowledge about the stock you are interesting in as well as the broad trends on the stock market at the time you want to buy. In other words, you should do your homework properly. Contrary to the notion that investing in stocks is only for experts, more and more ordinary people become interested in and informed about stocks. Nowadays there are so many stock investing guides (hard copies, ebooks and online products) that anyone can learn how the stock market operates, how to select good stocks to buy, how to manage them and why and when to sell them. To many individuals stock market investing has become a hobby.

Websites

A good place to start when gathering information about penny stocks is the internet. Not only will you find websites with valuable information about the economy in general, the oil and gold price, interest rates, inflation rates, currency values, company news etc., but also sophisticated stock investing programs containing graphs of every stock and every sector of the stock market. These programs also enable you to use the two main tools to evaluate stocks: fundamental analysis and technical analysis. When you become acquainted with analysis of company results, you can find these results in newspapers and on the internet. A number of new penny stock online programs have demonstrated astonishing techniques to uncover the jewels among the heaps of trash. Of course tons of money cannot be guaranteed; but there are customers who have reported amazing results.

Newsletters and Forums

Some websites issue free regular penny stock newsletters. These newsletters contain priceless information about companies, stocks and methods to explore penny stocks and their underlying companies. Online penny stock forums where participants discuss the merits of a product are equally useful.

Customer Reviews

Similar to penny stock forums are customers' reviews on a topic posted on a website. In some cases the customer reviewers award ratings to the programs or books on offer. Here you can expect diverse opinions, and you have to use your own judgment to decide which reviews are more trustworthy and balanced than others.

Chapter 6: Penny Stocks: An Overview

In some countries, penny stocks are referred to as cent stocks. Indeed many economies have baptized this category of stocks different names. What is for a fact is that penny stocks refer to common shares of small public companies that trade at low prices per share. Normally, penny stocks are looked at in terms of their pricing. In the USA, the Securities and Exchange Commission (SEC) defines a penny stock as any stock that is trading at a price below $5. The definitions of what encompass a penny stock may differ in different markets with some considering any stock that is trading below $1 to be penny stock.

In the United States, any stock that is trading over-the-counter bulletin board (OTCBB) or on pink sheets is considered to be a penny stock. By pink sheets, we mean that these stocks do meet any specific requirement by the regulator SEC. They earn their name because initially these stocks were printed on pink sheets. It is easy to identify them as they end with the letters "PK". OTCBB will become clear to you as we progress.

It is also necessary that we are able to distinguish between small caps and penny stocks as the two terms are at times used interchangeably. Small caps refer to stocks that have small market capitalization, that is, between $250 million and $2billion. As I had pointed earlier, penny stocks are looked at in terms of their prices and not market capitalization. It should therefore be obvious to you that a stock can be a small cap without necessarily being a penny stock.

Penny stocks are portrayed by different media as the most risky stocks to invest in. However like other small caps, penny stocks provide unlimited potential as far as gains in the stock market is concerned. These positive aspects of penny stocks may at times far outweigh the negative aspects of these stocks. Let us consider the following compelling reasons why I always advise investors to take up the challenge of penny stocks investments with a lot of faith. Remember, sometimes to take a step of faith, you need a little nudge.

Penny Stocks Present You Huge Potential Gains

Many big companies and multinationals were once small micro companies. Think of Microsoft or perhaps Home Depot. Did any one foresee the today big Microsoft? I bet not many. If you had foreseen this in the 1980s, then even a small investment would have ballooned into an extravagant investment. That is what penny stocks offer you.

Large cap companies are often very near to their maturity if not already there with limited growth potential. The best way to look at small cap companies is to view them as small companies with small total values but very high growth potential unique only to them. For instance, take a company with a market capitalization of $3 billion and compare its growth potential to a company with a market capitalization of $400 million. Unless the large cap company wants to be bigger than the entire economy (I am yet to hear of such a scenario), it cannot keep growing at that rate. The small cap therefore has higher growth potential. If you are looking for companies that can double your investments, then your stopping point is penny stocks.

Penny Stocks Are Mostly Under Priced

This breed of stocks attracts minimal analyst coverage. This informational gap in this market makes penny stocks under-reported and remains undiscovered. Unlike the ordinary stock market that any given information quickly reflects in the pricing of the stocks, penny stocks are not very sensitive to information and are often underpriced. An individual investor like the one reading this book can therefore take advantage of this market inefficiencies and profit from this opportunity.

Penny Stocks Produce The Best Portfolio Impact

Any financial expert you meet will tell you that stocks are better considered as long term investments. Your investment adviser will also stress the importance of a well-diversified portfolio and will definitely caution you against putting your eggs in only one basket. What is for sure is that when considered as long-term investments, you lose the liquidity of your investments.

When caught up in this trap, then penny stocks can be your only remedy. They allow you to increase your liquidity since they are subject to change and are better for short-term investments. Additionally, penny stocks allow you to spread your investments in many stocks and build a stronger portfolio.

Penny Stocks Are Lowly Priced

Coming to think of it like a layman, this low price of a penny stock would allow many individual investors to venture into the stock market. Looking at it in the perspective of financial economics, this means that you are not going to tie huge amounts of money in your investments and this is very good on a budget. It is even much bigger and better that in the unfortunate event that something happens against your hopes, you stand to lose less per share as compared to when the same event strikes your stocks that are pricier.

Do not forget also that the low cost of these stocks gives you the only opportunity to proudly own more stocks than the same amount would give you if you were investing in highly priced stocks. Isn't that good considering the high growth potential of these companies?

Penny Stocks Are Mostly Free From Institutional Investors

Most mutual funds do not invest in penny stocks. They would not want to risk their members' funds in companies that are still looking for their bearing. In most cases, institutional investors like mutual funds invest in over 20% of a company's stocks. The effected is highly inflated stock prices. If you are in the USA, SEC places tight regulations to funds that technically knock them out when it comes to establishing a position in the small cap market. This offers individual investors that are able to spot a promising company and get in before the giant investors mostly institutions come in. When these institutional investors come in, you will not be able to flex your muscles.

I know with these five key reasons for investing in penny stocks, you are almost convinced that this is the new direction. Good for you. However, investing in penny stocks without much investment knowledge and thought can be one of the worst investment mistakes you will ever commit. Like any investment vehicle you might think of, it is never a walk in the park. The very nature of these stocks makes them risky. But what really makes people perceive penny stocks riskier than their counter parts? These are outlined below:

The Penny Stock Market Is Very Volatile

We have said previously that penny stocks offer you the opportunity to double or even triple your investments within a short time. I avoided telling you then that they also offer you the opportunity to lose your investments overnight. My investment partner says that penny stock trade is where millions of gains and losses have equal probability.

The reason why small cap companies are susceptible to volatility is because of their low price. From an investor's point of view, this low price may mean that the company is in financial distress or perhaps is soliciting funds to salvage itself from an impending bankruptcy. The company could be offering stocks as a last-ditch effort to pay its debts and avoid dissolution. Even if the company is not in financial distress, it could mean that the company is less known or well established and there are no sufficient reasons to believe it will make it in the market. Needless to tell you, low price may mean low demand and hence compromise your liquidity position. You will have not many to sell your stock at favorable price.

Small volumes can greatly change prices for the penny stocks unlike with the large caps. It is not perplexing then for the penny stocks to move by 5% in a single trading day.

Penny Stock Market Is Not Regulated

Penny stock market is not as much regulated as compared to large cap markets. There are no criteria that a company should follow to be able to trade in the penny stock market. These companies are not required to provide their investors with their financial information and therefore investors lack credible information that can inform their financial decisions. This really tampers with investors' decisions and is a major cause of failed investments. You should however, go beyond the lamentation and employ the techniques I will share with you in this book to discard this informational asymmetry. It does not hold water for a serious investor.

Rogue Investors Have Found Their Way Into Penny Stock Market

The fact that the penny stock market is less regulated has made it easy for unscrupulous investors to defraud innocent investors. Unsuspecting investors are subjected to half-truths and outright lies. The results are penny stock traders who are penniless. It is easy for an unethical broker in the penny stock market to promise you double return even where less than a digit return is oblique. However, with this tutorial, you should put your worries aside because in this book, I tell you how to shift chaff from the grains.

The above section was meant to give you an overview on what you are about to venture into. What comes out clearly from the discussion is that even though penny stocks are portrayed by different people and media as highly risky, the truth is that they offer unlimited potential gains. Just how to make these gains while managing the downside potential a reality is the dilemma for many investors.

Chapter 7: How To Start?

Before going into the world of trading, even on pennies, you have to have the understanding of how the system works. How the highs and lows recur and most importantly, how can you use surf the tips of the curves to get profit out of it.

Getting into the actual trade is very easy. You can call your broker right now and ask from certain shares and that'd be it. You could be a shareholder in minutes. Or you could use the internet, register on one of hundreds of applications available and voila, you got yourself into trading.

But this convenience is one of the major reasons people lose their investments and by extension, their prosperous future plans to the market. You see, 95% of the penny stock market loses to the top 5%. That is because the top 5% are people who have carefully analyzed the market, know which stocks are most probable to rocket up and which are more tilted towards a complete collapse. It's easy to understand if you know how. We will teach you that a little later.

The most rational thing for you to do at this point of your career as a day trader is to dummy trade. Paper trade or online is your call. What dummy trading does is that it allows you to mingle with real stocks but with imaginary money. It's a perfect place for a beginner to start. Virtual trading software can act as a sandbox for your career. You can easily test out new strategies without risk of losing money and can get familiarity and experience of the stocks itself. Apps such as Tradacity, ThinkOrSwim and MarketWatch are good options for this purpose.

Some critics also argue that since you don't have the fear of losing or excitement of gaining while virtual trading, this method is a time-waste. It's not true. Without a risk of losing or gaining, the trading mind rarely gets out of the comfort zone and it's essential for you to understand each and everything about trading before you go inside the real world. For sure, the rules will be slightly different, the market activity will be different but essentially, the penny stock system is the same.

Spend some time on virtual trading until you feel comfortable with investing. This means understanding the way penny stocks work and the familiarity with the volatility of the stocks. With enough 'fake' trading, you'll be able to forge your own style and develop your own likes and dislikes about trading. Once you get to know yourself, your impulses would be a little easier to control which would in turn make you a more probable person to succeed because you would have decided by then, the best sources of information, the best stocks and the best strategy. Setup a starting cash amount and a reasonable time frame and keep iterating your inputs and outputs until you understand the ropes.

Chapter 8: A Quick Penny Stocks Vocabulary Lesson

You may have heard of penny stocks from a friend, read an article about it in the net or skimmed over an ad in your mail; whichever way you may have heard of it, it is undeniably an attractive and promising way of earning money that it deserves not only a second look but also a big long stare.

Put simply, a penny stock venture is a good way of getting money without having to give out a huge amount. In other words, it is easy money. But as simple as it sounds, dealing with penny stocks is a complicated business. After all, it still belongs to the world of business and stocks. And for a beginner like you, the terms will be enough to make your nose bleed.

Complicated as it is, there is no reason to fret. There is nothing like a quick and easy vocabulary review to help you get a good grip on stock trading terms.

The following words are the ones you will most likely encounter in your future penny stock trading venture and some are also used in this book. Every term is accompanied with an easy to understand meaning and description for your benefit.

Ask price or Sell price – the value of money that penny stock investors will get for the sale of their stocks.

Averaging down – a strategy in penny stock trading where you buy additional shares of the penny stocks that you already are in possession of. The good thing about this is that you can get the shares at a lesser price because of the slowly dropping value of the penny stock.

Bid price or Buy price – the value of money that penny stock investors will have to give to purchase a stock.

Change – the value that stands for the difference between the closing price of the day before and the value of the last trade.

De-listing – this occurs when a stock is not traded in a bulletin board or stock exchange anymore. This can be because the stock was not able to fulfill the requirement of the bulletin board or stock exchange that it has been traded in. Another reason would be that stock has transferred to a different exchange to be traded there. Also, there are situations where the stock has been taken by other organizations.

Fundamental analysis – the same as 'general research' (as discussed in Chapter 5).

Halts – a halt occurs when a stock exchange prevents a stock from being traded, sometimes as demanded by the company themselves. There are several reasons why a stock needs to be stopped from trading. The first, which is also the most common cause, is for certain information about the stock to have time to be spread and communicated, with the intention of affecting the value and price of the shares.

Hedging – another kind of penny stock trading strategy. The goal for this is to get different kinds of investments, the nature of which can be contrasting, so that when an event in the economy will decrease the performance of the first stock, the other stock will not be affected or, in some cases, improve.

Last Trade – indicated by the price and time of the transaction of the latest trade for a stock for a specific day.

Limit orders – specifying the price for every share that you will trade with.

Market capitalization – represents the value of the company. It can be calculated by multiplying the company's number of shares and the price for each of the share.

Market orders – executing a buy or sell order without specifying the share price.

Microcap stock fraud – this involves fraudulent activities related to the stocks of what is referred to as microcap companies. These are companies that have under $250,000,000 as their market capitalization.

NASDAQ Small Cap – this is the division of NASDAQ that penny stocks are also traded in. This is where small companies with share prices fewer than 5 dollars trade in, especially those that do not fulfill the requirements of NASDAQ.

Over the counter bulletin boards – a quotation service that regulates over the counter stocks or securities.

Over the counter stocks – these are stocks that are not traded in larger and more strictly regulated stock exchanges. This includes stocks that are unlisted in NASDAQ.

Partial fill – this occurs when you wanted to trade a specific number of shares, but in the end you didn't get to buy or sell the desired number. Unfortunately, partial fills can still cost you the same commission fee as that of a filled order.

Pink Sheets – a quotation publisher that also shows registered stocks' quotation information. Beginners should avoid trading in Pink Sheets as this is very risky and tricky.

Screening of stocks – this refers to the process done by investors like you to create a short list of stocks from an originally longer prospective list. The process of sorting out depends on the factors that you want to take into consideration, such as the share price, volume, and more. This can help you narrow down which stocks can be profitable for you.

Securities Exchange Commission (SEC) – a branch of the government that is responsible for the protection of investors, customers, and creditors. They ensure that all companies and brokers abide by their set rules and regulations to avoid illegal acts and malpractice in their trades.

Share volume – refers to the number of shares that are traded.

Short selling – another strategy of penny stock trading. Short selling a stock means selling it, but then intending to purchase them soon after.

Spread – this refers to the differences in the buy and sell price.

Stock quote – this basically refers to the price of a specific stock as it is quoted in a stock exchange. This specifically refers to the buy price, sell price, last-traded price, and the number of volume that the stock is traded.

Ticker symbol – the trading symbol with which organizations are identified with in the stock exchanges and bulletin boards.

Trade-order duration – the length of time that you want a buy order or a sell order to last and take effect. In executing a buy or sell order, you have the option of setting this duration. If you did not set trade-order duration, it will no longer be active at the end of the same day of trading that you executed the order, regardless if they are filled or unfilled.

Chapter 9: What Are Penny Stocks?

This is a book about trading penny stocks or "penny stocking". Penny stocking is simply the process of trading penny stocks. A penny stock is a stock that trades at a relatively low price and market capitalization compared to most stocks. Penny stocks typically trade outside of the major market exchanges. These types of stocks are generally considered to be highly speculative and high risk. There a number of reasons why penny stocks are considered to be higher risk than other types of securities. The main reasons are because of their lack of liquidity, large bid-ask spreads, small capitalization and limited following and disclosure. Penny stocks will often trade over the counter through the OTCBB and pink sheets.

Why choose this type of stock instead of the bigger, more established ones? Forget about stock market trading based on investing in big, established companies for long periods of time. That is not what penny stocking is all about. Penny stocking is about moments, not long years of wait and perseverance. It is a "get in and get out fast" type of trading.

Penny stocking is about surfing the speculative waves. What does this mean? Penny stocks are meant to be bought and sold quickly. It is about the investor purchasing great quantities of stocks and selling them as soon as they rise in value, generating significant profit in a matter of hours or days.

The most important thing to have in order to gain profit from this process is learning how to read the "waves". In order to be a great investment surfer the most important factor is understanding penny stocking as a game and not as a life long investment. A great poker player can make millions of dollars and a penny stocker is more akin to a gambler than to an investor.

It is very important never to forget the previous paragraph, it will make the difference between cashing in and cashing out successfully vs. just throwing your money away. Now, it is important to learn how to play. In all my years as a penny stock investor I have seen great success as well as great moments of disappointment. The group of failures I have seen have something in common: About 90% of people who lose money with penny stocking state that they never felt they knew all the "rules" of the game. They dove in the water without taking sufficient time to read the waves.

We all have lost a few bucks every now and then in some investment, but in the end the important thing is that the balance gets written in green. Everybody always asks me if it is really possible to make a good profit trading penny stocks. Well, the answer is "Yes". But it is important to study and apply the rules of market. This is the only way to turn $5000 into hundreds of thousands or more. I will proceed to give away my theories to help you develop an efficient market strategy in this book. A lot of people think it is a matter of fate, however, it is not fate what will make you money. It is skill, timing, and knowledge that will give you that fancy lifestyle you have always wanted.

The truth is that there are very few single transactions that can make you hundreds of thousands of dollars and it is important to keep that in mind, as many people lose the opportunity to gain as much as 500% from their investments in hopes of making even more profit by the end of the next day and having the unpleasant surprise that their stocks lost value in a matter of hours. It is important to understand that lots of the transactions will not generate profit beyond a few thousand dollars, but it is the constant game and observation that will allow a constant money flow straight to your pocket and one of the first rules I want you to learn is that penny stocks can generate a lot of money, but there are a few conditions to consider.

A lot of people learn their lessons in the worst way possible, losing loads of money, and the main purpose of this book is to save you that fate. By reading this, it is possible that you wonder if those are dangerous investments and I do not mean to send you to war without warning: They are. They are dangerous. In fact, everything is dangerous, from a bus ride to nightclubbing, so it is important for you to give yourself time to learn what penny stocks are in order to understand them, to see beyond your nose when it comes to converting your savings to stocks.

Penny stocks give you possibilities of profit and risk, in no way than other types of investment. How do I reduce risk? There is a single way: Reading. Faithful and careful reading of the economic media, dedication to detail regarding your investments. This is the only way of reducing great risks and effectively increase your profit, as you evade the commissions assumed by a stockbroker and also you would not depend on their knowledge or honesty, which is a very important factor when investing.

Here you encounter one of the axioms that are the key to my success: Depending on my insight and knowledge, as with enough attention I can have the same or more knowledge than the average stockbroker. To trade this type of stock you do not need a licensed stockbroker and my belief is that you do not need to work through one. Penny stocks are unique investments that do not require the sort of supposed knowledge and expertise that comes from a stockbroker. Your own analysis of the stock, the company, and the current state of the relevant sector(s) of the economy is much more important. This allows anyone the opportunity to be a successful investor if they are willing to take the time to learn. Few are the individuals who make a living out of penny stocking and even less the companies that dedicate themselves to it.

In this guide I will lay bare the blueprint for what I hope will be many successful years of penny stocking.

Chapter 10: Negative Situations

There are negative situations and events that can adversely affect the price of the stock. This chapter will teach you to be able to discern negative situations that are developing. By reading this chapter you will recognize events that can negatively impact the value of a penny stock.

Companies looking to bring up the price of their shares will often resort to doing reverse splits. In a reverse split the number of shares are reduced by a pre-selected factor. The ownership stake of the shares remains the same. A company having a 100 for 1 reverse split is diminishing the number of outstanding shares by 100. The new number of shares outstanding is now 100 times less than it previously was. The new share still retains the ownership percentage that 100 shares previously did. The price of the new stock reflects the number of shares it has taken the place of. If the old stock was worth .03

the new stock will be worth $3.00 since it is comprised of 100 old shares. You are now holding 1000 shares valued at $3000 where before you were holding 100,000 shares valued at $3,000. Your cost basis for the shares is still the same and the value of the shares will initially be the same.

The problem is that investors do not have faith that the stock will retain the higher price. They know that the stock is a penny stock with penny stock fundamentals. The company has not developed to the point where the stock would naturally reach the $3 price range. Investors start selling the stock, causing other investors to sell their stock, resulting in what is 90% of the time a large price decrease.

The other reason that investors start selling the stock is because they know that the company now will be issuing more shares into the market. The company has fewer shares outstanding so it can issue more shares. The shares are also worth more money now so the company will quickly move to take advantage of the opportunity to use their higher valued stock. The former penny stock can now issue 10,000 shares for allot more than it could before. The shares can be used to make acquisitions and allow the company not to have use as many shares as it would have had to in the past. The new shares that are used will further dilute the number of outstanding share in the market and bring down the price.

You should never buy or hold a stock that has announced or will soon be announcing a reverse split. There is a chance that the stock could increase in value after the split if the company has an outstanding development that provides a reason to support the higher price.

Penny stocks that are in bankruptcy will drastically fluctuate in price as the bankruptcy process moves on. The price fluctuation results from investors misunderstanding the bankruptcy process. When they hear that the company has obtained bankruptcy protection they assume that it means that the company is now protected against further financial harm. All bankruptcy protection means is that the company cannot be pursued by creditors and that a repayment plan will either be set up or the company will be reorganized. The company can still be liquidated if it no longer has the cash to operate. Or the bankrupt company can simply cease doing business and close up shop. Caldor filed for bankruptcy and then moved on to be liquidated. The stock trades on the pink sheets for .001 a share down from the .50 price range when it first announced that it had filed bankruptcy. Public companies, like private businesses, after going bankrupt often cease doing business instead of trying to reorganize. Once they cease doing business their stock is worthless.

The reason this happens is because bondholders and creditors receive proceeds from the liquidation of the company before common equity holders do. The stockholders will only be compensated after the bondholders and creditors have received the money owed to them. But since in a bankruptcy the bondholders and creditors will have to settle for as low as .20 on the dollar, there is no money left over for common stock holders.

Many investors think that reorganization means that they will receive stock in the new company. They buy the stock since they believe that they are buying into a turn around situation. Unfortunately they are mistaken and soon lose their entire investment.

Micro cap companies vary in the products and services that they offer. Many micro cap companies focus on standard products and established markets. Numerous micro caps focus on new untested products and what they perceive as being new emerging markets. When deciding on which micro cap to invest you in you want to be able to research the market for the product. The newer and untested the product is the harder it will be research its potential.

A new product is fine as long as its market is established. A new computer device can be profitable if there already is a market for it. But the same computer product would not be a hit in a country with a very low computer usage rate. Make sure that there is a demand for the penny stock's product.

Many micro caps have products for which they plan on creating a market for. They might develop a device that can detect when milk is spoiled. While people might be concerned with being able to know if the milk is spoiled or not, they can resort to the old-fashioned smell test. This product although advanced and useful would have no practical market since people do not need a device to measure the freshness of milk. The company would have to convince people somehow that they are better off using a $10 device for an action that they can do for free now. I am sure you can see how quickly both the product and company would fail.

Be wary of investing in penny stocks that sell products that are not tested and for which there is no demand. People buy products that fill a need. They do not products when they do not have a need for them.

Hot tips are a source of trouble. Investors receive hot tips from friends, relatives, and business associates. The tip itself is not the problem. Very often the tips are valuable and the stock's they concern do go up. The problem with hot tips is that most often by the time you get it the whole world has had time to react to the same information you were given. The information originates from an original source that passes the tip down to a few selected individuals who pass it down to their friends who pass it on again until the full cycle is repeated. The issue that I have with hot tips is that you never know how far down you are in the chain. If you are the 100th person to receive the tip chances are that the stock has already been bought up and the price reflects the information. If the tip comes out to be true there will be selling from the investors who bought the stock before you. By the time you buy it people might be getting ready to sell the stock.

The other problem with buying a stock based on a hot tip is that you are deviating from your investment strategy. You are not buying the stock based on your research and your money is at the mercy of a tip that may be wrong. You can make the right investments based on your research without having to rely on other people's advice.

Government investigations always have adverse effects on penny stocks. The investigation can conclude with the company being cleared. But by the time the company is cleared and the investigation is complete the name of the company will have been dragged through the mud. Investors will read about what the reason the government is investigating the company and assume that the penny stock is guilty as charged. Penny stocks have a bad reputation to begin with so it will not take much to ruin the reputation of a penny stock.

Consumer backlash against a company is even worse than a government investigation. A government investigation will either find the company guilty or innocent of the suspected wrongdoing. Once a company has been found to be innocent investors will slowly return. It can take years for them to come back but there is nothing preventing them from returning to the stock. Consumer backlash against a company is enormously damaging both to the company and to the stock. When consumers decide that they no longer trust the quality of a product or the competence of the company they will never use its products again. A company that manufactures defective car seats will never be able to over come the stigma resulting from an accident. Customers will never take a chance with their car seats because of what is at stake. The company will not sell any more car seats and its stock will crumble when earnings turn into losses.

Micro cap companies that are the focus of customer backlash do not have the benefit of sitting on a cushion of cash to help them pass through the difficult period. A large established company has enough cash to weather a storm. The micro cap cannot count on a press relations department to work the media. Once it becomes embroiled in a customer backlash period it can start counting its days.

The old-fashioned boiler room operation consisted of a row of phones manned by brokers with the job of calling investors and convincing them to buy a worthless a stock. The stock would appreciate in price and the boiler room operator would dump his shares to the unsuspecting investors. Boiler room victims were usually the elderly who are unfamiliar to investing and are by nature more trusting.

Today the boiler room operation has substituted the use of phones for the Internet. The Internet provides the tools to reach millions of investors with the push of a button. In the time that it used to take to call one investor, the boiler room operation can now send an email touting a stock to thousands of investors.

Other ways stocks are sold to unsuspecting investors under false premises is through the use of newsletters, emails, message boards, and chat rooms. A thinly traded stock is first bought up by a group of investors. Once they control the supply the start promoting it using every available means. The stock price increases sharply due to the lack of supply since the group controls the supply. Investors continue placing orders for the stock that is being marked up by the Market Makers due to the high demand and limited supply. When the stock is high enough the group dumps all their shares on the investors who soon discover that the information on the stock was fabricated and that the stock was manipulated.

Chapter 11: Successful Stock Traders Have Study Habits.

Knowledge is power, as they say. You do not go to war without studying the situation. You do not build a house without counting the cost. Don't go to stock trading without the right information. You need to study. You need to do research.

First, study what stock market is all about. Most of the time, when people hear the words stock market, they picture a group of people, all holding a phone with the left hand and holding a pen and a paper on the right hand, shouting at the top of their voices, looking at the giant overhead monitor, with signs of stress showing all over their faces? It's a picture of pure chaos. But is that the real picture of stock market?

So what is stock market? It is not equivalent to online casino wherein you can win huge amount of money or lose devastating amount of money, all by pure luck or bad luck. It is certainly not an invention of aliens. The language being used by the traders, though very confusing, is not derived from Mars, believe it or not.

Most people do not understand stock trading (if you are one of them, then congratulations, you are normal). This what makes it intimidating to many. People usually define stock trading based on the experiences of the people they know or what is in the news. For example, Mr. A lost a million or Mrs. B gained a million, in stocks. They would base their decision whether to join or not on the account of one experience of another person.

Simply put, a stock trade occurs when a certain company or organization needs money for the business. They can actually borrow (to lending companies) or sell stock (a share of the ownership of the business). Selling a share is more advantageous for the founders of the business because there is no loan interest plus there is no pressure to return the money to the traders or investors. The only commitment is as co-owners, the traders have now a share also to the profits of the said company, if ever there would be profits (there is no 100% guarantee though). So the more shares they have, the more their capacity to earn. Be warned though, the same applies to losses.

Highly successful traders therefore take the time to study the profile of the company they want to invest in. They consider the fluctuations of the market, the strategies to use and the risks involved. They are also open to new events or happenings and to the changing trends. They study all the angles before they make the decision.

One habit as a stock trader that you need to develop is the habit of getting all the facts first before deciding on an investment. Do not just rely on hearsays.

Wise investors would tell the new ones to never invest in a business that they do not know. Make a journal. This is effective in recording the ups and downs of your investment. Document also the winnings and the losses. Do your homework. Study, research, review and then take the plunge, invest!

Chapter 12: Getting Started With Penny Stocks

Now that you know all the terms, let's get you started with other basic requirements. Here are some things that you will need to trade in penny stocks successfully.

A computer

First is a computer. Although you can consider getting a laptop, it would be best to work with a desktop. A desktop will give you an office feeling and you won't have to worry about lugging your laptop around. You can set up an office, in fact, and prevent others from using the room.

A desktop computer is generally also more secure, because you don't take it with you to public places. If you need to trade on the go, there are plenty of apps available that will connect you to the information found on your desktop computer, so you don't need to worry about mobility. Even so, make sure that you password protect all the devices that you use for stock trading.

Reliable connection

I cannot stress this point enough. Technology has revolutionized stock trading in the last couple of decades and online trading has become almost the exclusive method of stock trading. You cannot deal in stocks if you don't have an Internet connection. In fact, you cannot deal in penny stocks if you don't have a reliable and fast Internet connection. As you know, the penny stock market is extremely volatile and will fluctuate rapidly. If you end up missing something, you will have to settle for a loss. Every second counts in the penny stock market, so it is best to invest in a fast and reliable Internet connection.

Once again, buying and selling stocks is much like attending an auction. It requires your complete attention; otherwise an opportunity may slip through your fingers.

Besides reliable Internet, it is also not a bad idea to have some sort of power backup ready. If you were to lose power, everything you were doing could be lost if you didn't save it in time and you may miss out on some great opportunities. Getting a back-up battery for your desktop computer is a cheap and easy way to avoid this problem.

Trading account

Although you have to buy and sell penny stocks over the counter, you might still need a trading account to trade in penny stocks. For this, you can open an account in a trading firm. The firm needs to be trustworthy and you can check their background before opening up an account with them. Keep in mind that fees vary greatly from broker to broker. There are usually subtle differences in trading firm guidelines, as well, so make sure you do your research before you decide on the one you want.

The procedure to open the account is generally quite simple: You only have to fill out details and provide them with a few required documents in order to complete the legal requirements. Once your account is up and running, you can get started with the trading.

Broker

The next step is to employ a broker, who will be able to guide you through the correct steps. This is an especially important step if you are new to penny stocks and don't know how to go about things. A broker will have access to all the right information and will be able to guide you properly. You have to find a good one, though, and do a background check if possible. Your broker should have experience and should have dealt with penny stocks. He or she should also be a qualified broker with proper certification. Going through a financial firm to find a broker is probably the best thing to do, as you will find an ideal one.

Budget

Next, decide upon a budget. You have to set a budget that will help you invest the right amount in the market. You need to look at a sum that will be enough to get you started with penny stocks. Don't set a very high budget. Penny stocks are low-priced stocks that range between $5 and $10, which means you don't need a big budget for it. You can keep adding in money as and when you think right to do so.

This step is extremely important, as you don't want to get in over your head. Set a daily limit of what you can invest and stick to it. You should never decide to exceed your budget unless it is a special circumstance. If you are married, having a budget will also show your spouse that you are being responsible. If you want to go over your limit, talk about it first with your broker or an advisor.

Research

You have to conduct due research on the topic in order to invest wisely. Your research should pertain to understanding the basics of penny stocks, what they can do for you, how they will contribute to your portfolio, how safe they are, etc. Besides just looking at financial news, also consider general national news. Current events can influence the market just as much as the history of a company or the state of local affairs. In short, you will need to be a well-rounded individual who keeps up with the times in order to be a successful penny stock trader.

Once you finish the basic research, you can move to researching the best stocks to invest in. Not all stocks in the penny category will be wise choices and you have to pick the ones that you think are doing well at the current moment. Once you finalize a few, you can pick out the best from that lot.

Make sure you get advice, especially when choosing your first stocks. Once you gain some experience you may also feel comfortable buying or selling stocks without consulting someone else first, but this should be the exception rather than the rule. Someone else's experience can help you just as much, if not more than your own head knowledge.

Message boards

The next thing to consider looking into is message boards. Message boards are places where people post messages about good stocks that they wish to suggest. These suggestions are meant to help people make their decisions on which stocks to buy and which ones to avoid. You can look at which stocks are trending and which are not doing well. There will be both pumpers and bashers on the forum. The former will promote a good stock by asking people to buy it whereas the latter will bash a stock thereby bringing down its value. You have to study the boards for a while to see who is genuinely suggesting good stocks and how they are doing in the market.

Make sure that you are a part of several different types of message boards in order to get a well-rounded view of the market. Online chat groups, Facebook groups, and local community groups are great options, just to name a few.

Journal

It is important for you to maintain a journal in order to write down all your experiences in the stock market. Keep a record of your investments from the stocks that you pick to the money invested to any other information that you think needs to be recorded. You can choose a digital or physical diary for the journal. You must dedicate yourself to making the entries in order to keep a consistent record. Looking back at the journal will help you avoid making any mistakes and remain on the right path.

Make sure you make an entry every time you sell or buy a stock. Try to organize your journal so it is easy to follow. Dividing it into sections for each type of investment, from penny stocks to precious metals, is a good place to start. Beyond that, highlight any types of stocks you seem to be doing well in. Looking at your journal, you will hopefully be able to see any emerging patterns in your successes as compared to your losses, which will help point out things that you should avoid.

These are the various things to look into when you wish to start trading in penny stocks. Armed with these tools, you are in great shape to jump right in. Next we will take a look at what exactly makes penny stocks tick.

Chapter 13: Pink Sheet Trading And Its Profitability

Pink sheets are an OTC market that connects broker-dealers electronically—everything, including price quotes, are done virtually. There is no trading floor required. However, because of the virtual environment pink sheet trading has to offer, it differs from the New York Stock Exchange (NYSE). The required criteria for pink sheet-listed companies aren't the same as the required criteria for companies listed on the NYSE. Because of these innate differences, you'll want to spend some time familiarizing yourself with the nature of pink sheets. That is what we are going to discuss in the following chapter—the securities, benefits, risks, and profitability ratios pink sheet trading has to offer to investors in pursuit.

Who Can Be Pink Sheet-listed?

Generally speaking, you'll find that most pink-listed companies are small companies either starting out or struggling to obtain positive profit margins. They're typically thinly traded, tightly held companies. For the struggling company especially, pink sheet trading is a bonus—companies that are pink sheet-listed don't need to meet or maintain any particular requirements in order to obtain or remain pink sheet-listed. All an interested company needs to do is submit a Form 211 with the OTC Compliance Unit, with current financial information included, in order to be listed. That's it, no strings attached.

You should know that when you delve into the world of pink sheet trading, you'll find that some companies eagerly and willingly show you their financial books—their financial records, so to speak—while others don't. Unfortunately, pink sheet-listed companies are not obligated or required to show you their books upon request. You'll also inevitably encounter problems with finding annual reports on pink sheet-listed companies that interest you, since these companies don't file annual or periodic reports with the Securities and Exchange Commission (SEC). Unfortunately for the investor—you—this makes it nearly impossible to gain *all* the necessary financial information regarding a company of interest (unless they're willing to give it to you, of course).

The Difference between Pink Sheets and OTCBB

Whereas OTCBBs, a topic we learned about in the previous chapter, are owned and operated by NASDAQ, pink sheets are owned by private companies. And because OTCBB is organized by NASDAQ, the second largest exchange platform in the world, it makes sense that strict rules, regulations, and standards follow. It's compulsory for issuers, for example, to register with the Securities and Exchange Commission. No registration is required for pink sheet-listed companies, nor do such rules or regulations exist.

The Benefits of Pink Sheets

Pink sheets can be extremely cheap per share, some costing less than a dollar even. This makes pink sheet trading highly beneficial and incredibly advantageous to the potential investor looking to invest in small increments but interested in reaping potentially high financial rewards. Volatility levels are very high with pink sheets, so increases in even *penny* amounts may result in great financial returns for an investor.

If you're looking to reap dramatic benefits, and are willing to take oftentimes bold financial risks in order to do so, you might want to look for companies that have recently suffered from negative financial events, but have the potential to make a comeback. Companies that were once listed on the NYSE, for example, might be a good starting point—you can purchase shares from the company and wait—and hope—that it makes a comeback.

One of the great things about pink sheet-listed companies is that you can invest your money in a small or unpopular company, but still achieve a positive return rate. If a company is small and less known, you have a higher chance of success because the competition is low. Investing in these small companies could turn out to be quite profitable if the growing process continues over time. In the future, and with gradual growth, that same company might even end up on a major exchange.

The Risks of Pink Sheets

As an investor, you should be well aware that there can be many disadvantages to pink sheet trading as well, especially when investment opportunities and endeavors are approached in inappropriate or unknowledgeable ways. As you may have guessed by now, based on our earlier conversation, one of the biggest disadvantages of pink sheet trading is the limited amount of information that listed companies are required to share with investors and dealer-brokers. A company's decision to not report their financial status or publish annual reports makes it more difficult for investors to gain the knowledge they need to consider the company, make vital financial decisions, and take risk-free actions. In other words, without these annual reports, you will not have all the crucial information about what you are purchasing and how the company doing.

These pink sheet-listed companies are also thinly traded. You can purchase 500 shares from a company that promises to become the next Microsoft, but what happens if you gain a good profit and then decide to sell? When you sell, the price of the stock goes down. When large numbers of investors continually do this, stocks and companies gain the title of being thinly traded. Regardless of what the market is when you do decide to sell, if you don't find a potential buyer for your stocks, you will not be able to get out of the position you put yourself in.

This situation becomes even more complicated when it comes to pink sheet-listed companies. It is a hard task to initiate a stock position when the bid-ask spreads are high. If you want to invest in those companies, you should be aware of the fact that they usually may not be covered by analysts. For example, if you watch or read the daily financial news, you will already know that they almost never cover companies that are not listed on a major exchange. This means that you will have to do some extra research in order to stumble upon the important information you need to make knowledgeable decisions and take successful actions.

The Workings of the Pink Sheet Tier System

I mentioned the tier system synonymous with the pink sheet trading system earlier, but let's stop for a second and take a closer look before moving on. In recent years, the pink sheet system has adopted something called "market tiers," an organizational method that lists and separates the companies who have higher risk levels from those with lower degrees of financial risk. With these tiers, you gain a sense of increased clarity regarding the type of company you are investing in. As its name suggest, there are certain levels, or tiers, that a company can fall under. There are five in total, which you'll soon discover in the following section:

Tier #1: Trusted tiers. Just like their name suggest, these tiers are confirmed by the pink sheet OTC market to be trustworthy and highly appealing to investors seeking to invest. The companies that fall under this tier have both international and United States companies. With this in mind, the trusted tier can then be divided into two sub-categories, as follow:

International Premier QX: These consist of overseas companies that are listed on an exchange that is international, though they still cover the required financials of the listed worldwide standards noted and regulated by the NYSE. These companies conduct an independent audit and are able to present an immediate CEO certification to anyone who refuses to comply with corporate governance.

Premiere QX: This includes companies that are based only in the US and continually meet the standards of the NASDAQ's capital market. It is not necessary for those companies to report to the SEC, although they still have to follow the requirements that NASDAQ lists.

Tier #2: Transparent Tiers. This tier is immediately below the trusted tier and consists of:

OTCBB pink quotes: This represents companies that are listed on both the OTCBB and pink sheet systems. OTCBB makes it necessary for these companies to give frequent reports to the SEC.

OTCBB: As you've learned throughout this book already, these companies are simply listed on the OTCBB market only.

Information right now: These are the companies that have daily and current information, meaning that they provide the given information with the OTC Disclosure or the Securities and Exchange Commission. The information that is provided is less than 6 months old. If a company wants to keep itself up on this exact tier and not move down, it needs to file an annual report within the period of 75 days after the ending of the final quarter. The information will be verified as posted by the pink sheets OTC market.

Tier #3: Distressed Tiers. These are the next on the tier and are tough to manage. The companies listed within this tier include:

Companies with limited information:

The information that is listed may be available for everyone to view, but it is generally older than 6 moths and often doesn't meet the pink sheets OTC market requirements.

A company might file a report to the SEC, but they still haven't kept that report updated frequently.

Broken and bankrupted companies oftentimes pop-up on this list. These companies must promptly file information with both the News Service and OTC Disclosure.

Tier #4: Only two kinds of companies are included in the **Defunct Tiers**:

Companies without information: This category can be easily recognized by its stop signal sign. Companies that fall under this tier are either defunct or haven't filed any kind of update on current information to the OTC Disclosure, the Securities and Exchange Commission, or the News Service in the last 6 months. If you are considering any investment into these types of companies, proceed with caution.

Gray Markets: This second market, much like the previous tier category, has its own symbol, too—the exclamation point. The companies listed in the gray market are missing a market maker and are not listed on both OTCBB and pink sheets. As a bonus, there is no market transparency.

Trades in the gray market are created by a broker-dealer and are reported to the SRO, who tracks prices.

Tier #5: Toxic tiers, just like its name indicates, are tiers that have an extremely high-risk level. Its symbol, the skull and crossbones, suggests the risk investors take when pursuing companies listed within this tier. Only one category falls under this tier:

Caveat Emptor: The translation of this tier's title to English is quite clear—"Buyer beware." On pink sheets, these tiers are described as stocks that can be a spam, have unclear promotion, undergo regular suspensions, and many others things that reveal their risk level. Many of the companies listed within this bottom most tier are all too often scams.

Now that you know a little more about the 5 types of tiers within the investing and penny stocks world, we need to talk about the brokers. That is, if you decide to invest in pink sheet stocks, you should consider hiring a broker. If you have already made a broker account, your broker will probably grant you an allowance to trade pink sheet stocks. Be wary, though, that this might not be possible, as some brokerage firms only allow their most loyal clients to trade in the pink sheet market. If you do find an opportunity to delve into the pink sheet trading market with the help of your broker, you will be asked to sign another form that states that you understand and agree that pink sheet stocks and their trading can be risky investment endeavors.

You should also know that there are many companies out there who simply don't want to give out information concerning their business and financial matters. Be careful in investing in companies that do this. Pink sheet companies are highly appealing due to their low price, and many investors find them interesting investment opportunities because they want to step up into a current and potentially rising company. The possibility that you may lose portions or all of your investment if you don't make the right buying choice means that you need to think carefully and think twice before proceeding with any decision.

You'll always want to avoid speculative stocks. Pink sheet trading has made major progress in the last few decades, and there have been more standards set and information circulating about pink sheet-listed companies, thanks to the OTC market's help. If a pink sheets-listed company is introduced to one of the tier systems we discussed earlier, the more likely an investor will find it attractive. Watch and pay attention to the tier system you select, and ask for professional help before making any financial decisions. Be wary of some of the "expert" advertisements, as many are unreliable or even scams. Sit down and do the research yourself. You can also take a look at the OTC Markets Group website. They have a detailed list of many OTC stocks. For now, though, you'll want to focus mostly on the two main stock categories—OTCQX and OTCQB. The other categories will not have that much information given and there may not be many strategies for them!

As this chapter winds down and comes to an end, here is a reminder of the topics and ideas we discussed throughout this chapter, and a list of a few important things you should remember about pink sheet stocks:

They are listed as nano-cap stocks.

No exchanges registered.

Pink sheet-listed companies usually have a very small record of their financial history, making it difficult for investors to identify past financial patterns and business models.

Most companies that are pink sheet-listed offer new stocks, so you won't be investing in already successful and thriving companies.

Most pink sheet-listed companies aren't required to file reports with the Securities and Exchange Commission.

It might be difficult to find reliable and helpful information about a pink sheet-listed company's current finances and economic standings

Delving into the realm of pink sheet trading makes you more susceptible to scams and fraud through faxes, e-mails, websites, mail, etc.

Pink sheet trading can be difficult to invest into unless you hire a broker to help you out professionally.

Pink sheet-listed companies tend to be very illiquid, making the buying and selling process a somewhat challenging endeavor.

Pink sheet-listed companies are thinly traded.

Chapter 14: Identifying Penny Stock Scams

It is difficult not to consider a penny stock which is being advertised as the next big thing. Although it can easily be considered a scam, a lot of new investors still fall into this trap. There are thousands of publicly listed companies in a major stock exchange. However, so many individuals are still drawn to lesser known penny stock companies.

A penny stock company listed on the Over-The-Counter Bulletin Board, an electronic system which shows real-time quotations, volume information, and last-sale prices of securities, is often advertised as being listed in NASDAQ. This is not completely true although NASDAQ oversees OTCBB. On the other hand, a penny stock listed on Pink Sheets isn't regulated by any financial organization or government entity. As such, it is a riskier investment than any other major stock company listed on a stock exchange. The company can post losses and deficits can be huge. Furthermore, it can easily fold up. An investor can check with the Securities and Exchange Commission for information regarding a penny stock company.

Tools And Strategies Used In Penny Stock Scams

Spam and junk emails can be distributed by scam artists to generate interest on a particular penny stock. In general, these emails contain fictitious information about the stock. It is highly advised not to buy the advertised stock just on the basis of emails received. In addition, online bulletin boards are used to spread "hot tips" about a certain stock. Scammers use aliases to spread false information. Again, any interest investor must practice due diligence when he intends to invest in a penny stock. Some of these companies also pay stock promoters to offer "unbiased and independent" recommendations through the mass media. Before believing these paid promoters, it is best to investigate if they have financial certifications.

Cold calls and boiler room tactics are also used by fraudsters who have an organized group of high-pressure sales agents. These agents make cold calls to encourage potential investors to buy the penny stock. It is advised to be careful about receiving calls from unknown people. Furthermore, the penny stock company may issue dubious press releases. The potential investor must make it a point to investigate the facts on his own so that he won't be scammed.

In case the individual is scammed, he can report the incident to his broker. If the latter doesn't resolve the issue, the former can report it to the Securities and Exchange Commission or the securities regulator of the state.

Why People Become Interested in Penny Stocks

A penny stock offers the possibility and excitement to become rich quickly. It is the same as a lottery ticket which offers a better future to the winner (if it's a winning ticket). An individual who invests in a penny stock is usually someone who doesn't perform mathematical computations to find out the penny stock company's intrinsic worth. He doesn't analyze financial statements, industry studies, dividend projections, or discounted cash flows. In addition, a penny stock is like hidden knowledge. An investor who has an interest in a certain stock often feels special because he knows something which the others don't know. If he talks about his investment, people will listen because it is something they haven't heard of.

A penny stock lacks liquidity. That's why a lot of experts don't recommend buying such a stock. However, it is also very volatile. This means the price may experience wild fluctuations which create a lot of opportunities to profit quickly. An inexperienced investor may continuously buy shares of the penny stock because the price continuously goes up. He doesn't realize that he is one of those people who drive up the price. In case he intends to sell his shares, he soon realizes that no one wants to buy the stock anymore. An investor decides to invest in a certain penny stock because he believes that this company is next Microsoft or the next Wal-Mart. He fails to recognize that these companies, which started from humble beginnings, offered shares to the public when they have grown large already. These companies opted for IPOs because they want to expand the business.

Actually, these investing traps can be avoided if the investor thinks of himself as the owner of the penny stock company. He has to take out his emotions from the investment equation in order to make a realistic and correct decision. Liquidity isn't even a problem if the penny stock company continuous to grow.

Considerations In Buying A Penny Stock

A lot of traditional investors have become rich because they have invested in high quality stocks. But only a few, if any, have become rich because of penny stock investing. The power of compounding consistent gains from high quality stocks is the single factor responsible for the enormous wealth of these traditional investors. Their chosen companies continuously grow in revenues and profits. These companies offer high returns for the investors' money. Dividends are often distributed to shareholders. Investors continuously buy shares to increase their earnings.

On the other hand, an investor in a penny stock company can't increase his shares because of liquidity problems. If he continuous to buy, he will cause the price of the share to increase. The penny stock is inefficient; therefore, an investor has to buy higher costs for every transaction. These costs reduce any profit an investor may earn from his investment. In fact, he may even lose money because of these frictional costs.

Chapter 15: Some Techniques & Strategies

Start With Swing Trading

You will want to start off your investment strategy with swing trades. Regardless if this is the approach that you ultimately end up using, starting off this way is a great entry point into the world of penny stocks. Using a swing trade approach you will be forced to look at whole exchanges as well as individual stocks. You will also be looking at the distilled information about these exchanges and stocks and wont' be concerned about underlying products or the prowess of CEOs and management. I suggest you use this perspective for at least a month. This will give you time to become acquainted with cycles and what they look like. I hope that this strategy works for you, but even if doesn't, the knowledge you will gleam from it is invaluable.

Don't Trust The Word Of The Company

When researching companies for a buy and hold strategy, or looking for undervalued stocks, the research materials that you consult will be very important. You will want to look at data that cannot be distorted by the company you are researching. This means that when trading on the Pink Sheets that you discount any information on a company's self filed financial reports, and on the NASDAQ and OTCBB it means that you are discounting the word of management and CEOs. This is especially true for a buy and hold strategy where you have the greatest chance of finding a company that has a real chance of going mainstream. It's these companies that tend to start putting out press releases and other bits of information about their company and their product. These press releases are always designed to put the company in the best possible light. You must never trust a single word on any of these reports.

I have yet to discover a company that I have had enough trust in to use a buy and hold strategy, but that doesn't mean I don't occasionally look at what companies are out there. I typically research new tech companies and it blows my mind the types of ridiculous exaggerations that make their way into company press releases. I've seen reports saying a famous programmer was joining the company, when in fact that programmer had just re-tweeted something from that company. I've seen companies state that they are six weeks from full product, and just months from being on store shelves. They were in fact six weeks away from a working prototype – one that ultimately ended up not working – their product never made its way to stores. The point is, these companies will say anything to keep you invested or to get you to invest more. Do your research but be aware of where this information is coming from. Always express doubt in a company and keep in mind that their survival depends on keeping you from selling their stock.

Keep A Detailed Log Of Your Trades

I mentioned earlier that before you start trading you will need a log book so you can try out some practice trading. In this notebook you will be analyzing your trades, making notes of why you bought a stock, how long you held onto a stock, and some information about the previous cycles that convinced you to buy. This is an exhaustive process, but analyzing our previous trades is the only way to get better. As you start to deal with real money and real trades, you will still want to continue updating your trade journal. You don't need to do this with every trade, but try analyzing every fourth of fifth trade you make in the same way that you did before any real money got involved.

Keep an investment journal. It is an invaluable tool and will help you realize your strengths and weaknesses.

Image courtesy of the aws.amazon.com

	A	B	C	D	E	F	G	H
1	Underlyin	Action	Quantity	Price	Time	Date	Exch.	Order Ref.
2	PNR	BOT	100	45.24	14:06:26	20121005	ARCA	ChartTrader1727371693
3	PNR	BOT	100	45.24	14:06:26	20121005	ISLAND	ChartTrader1727371693
4	MAR	SLD	100	38.46	14:16:42	20121005	CBSX	ChartTrader1052367072
5	MAR	SLD	20	38.46	14:16:42	20121005	BATS	ChartTrader1052367072
6	LPHI	BOT	200	2.65	15:23:52	20121005	BATS	ChartTrader1433330899
7	MTL	BOT	100	7.09	15:26:42	20121005	CBSX	ChartTrader1433330899
8	MTL	BOT	100	7.09	15:26:42	20121005	BEX	ChartTrader1433330899
9	FLEX	BOT	400	6.12	15:34:17	20121005	BEX	ChartTrader1433330899
10	FLEX	BOT	100	6.12	15:34:17	20121005	BYX	ChartTrader1433330899
11	DNKN	SLD	100	31	18:30:39	20121005	ISLAND	ChartTrader1433330899
12	DNKN	SLD	100	31	18:30:39	20121005	ISLAND	ChartTrader1433330899
13	DNKN	SLD	100	31	18:30:47	20121005	ISLAND	ChartTrader1433330899
14	DECK	SLD	50	36.24	19:32:19	20121005	ISLAND	ChartTrader12294249
15	IGT	SLD	200	12.88	19:39:55	20121005	NYSE	ChartTrader12294249
16	NXPI	BOT	100	25.29	19:55:42	20121005	ISLAND	ChartTrader1052367072

You will want to do more thorough review of your investments around every two months. A thorough review means looking down at a week by week breakdown of how your trading is going. Any broker that you end up using will be able to produce a print out of this week-by-week summary. I personally compare this printout to how the overall exchanges were doing, and to how the best stocks within an exchange were doing. This type of assessment tells you how you are doing relative to the market overall. You will be able to look at the trades that you made in a given week and compare it to the best picks and the market overall, giving you insight into what you did right and what you did wrong. When you combine this with your trade journal that has more insight into why you picked individual stocks and what cycles led you to pick these stocks, then suddenly you have an incredibly clear picture of what happened during that trading period.

Please make a practice of analyzing your past trades using the method outlined. I know that it is a lot of extra work, but it is through this reflection that I have become such a profitable trader. I never would have realized that, when looking for undervalued stocks, I have to stick with tech companies. I never would have realized this had I not created a journal and done this reflection. Don't think about analyzing your past trades as creating extra work for yourself – it is far more essential than that. Keep it in mind for every aspect of your trading career and you will find that you are making better and more consistent profits.

Don't Buy More Than 1/10 Of The Total Trades Of A Stock In A Given Day

This is a mathematical principle of penny stocks, and one that is fairly well known. You'll want to exhibit the same practice and never buy more than one tenth of the total trades of a stock in a given day. For example, if $10,000 of CISCO stock is traded per day on average, you do not want to end the day with more than $1,000 is CISCO stock. The mathematical proof for this is a little bit complicated but the concept is this: you know that these companies are extremely volatile and that's how you will make your money. You also know that a stock is unlikely to trade more than it does on average, in this case $10,000. This means that in the worst case scenario $10,000 of CISCO stock is offloaded before you have a chance to sell your $1,000. If that much stock ever got moved the value of what you are holding would plummet, but by not having more than 10% of the daily trade value, you insulate yourself from total wipeouts on a stock. In this case, a total wipeout is not wiping you investment fund, but wiping the value of the stock so low that you lose all of your money in a single stock.

The averages for how much a penny stock trades in a day can be pretty extreme. One week the volume could be as high as $10,000, and the next it might be $5,000. You will want to look at the average for a given week, and not the average over the lifetime of a stock. Even within a given week the volume of shares traded in a day can change very quickly. Use the last few days of trading data to establish your limits, but be aware of all the large changes in volume a company has had. If a stock seems unstable in how much it is being traded for, as in there is no good average that you can use, set a maximum between 5% and 8% of yesterday's trading volume.

Sales Pitch

Before I buy any stock, even if I only plan on holding onto it for a few hours, I always make a sales pitch to myself to determine if it's really worth buying. I love this technique because it forces me to distill why I'm buying a stock. Sales pitches are usually sixty seconds or less and you will have to think through your reasoning for buying a stock. Don't take more than a minute to create a sales pitch and convince yourself – you don't want the price to fluctuate too much. This method has saved me several times from making poor choices. For example, I was looking at a stock sometime last year and was going to purchase based on a series of cycles the stock was having. I was using the swing trade approach and it seemed like a simple trade – buy and hold onto it for two or three days and then sell. I was trying to convince myself on the stock and came to the realization that I should wait for the next cycle. This is because I picked up on the trend as the stock was picking up. It looked attractive initially, but giving it a little bit of thought through a condensed sales pitch led me to wait and buy later, making much more profit on the next cycle. Take a minute to try and convince yourself before you buy a stock – it only takes a moment and it could save you a fortune.

Chapter 16: Penny Stock Day Trading

In this chapter, we will look at what day trading stands for and why you should day trade with penny stocks. Day trading really is the easiest way to break into the penny stock world, and we hope this chapter helps you do just that.

What is day trading?

Day trading refers to trading that occurs within a single day. The investor will buy and sell stocks within the same day and not hold on to them, even if it means settling for a loss.

Now you may wonder why the trader is keen on disposing of the stocks when he can hold on to them for a while longer and ring in a profit.

The answer is quite simple: The trader is not interested in allowing his investment to remain where it will not prove to be a lucrative choice. He is better off taking a loss at that point in time than a profit on it sometime later, which will eventually prove to be a bigger loss.

For example, let's say an investor has bought 100 stocks worth $2 each. He has made an investment of $200, which he hopes to increase to $250 by end of the day. However, the per stock value drops to $1.5 at the end of the day, meaning that he has to settle for a loss.

The trader will agree to take the loss and will not hold the stock unnecessarily. Even if the stock moves to $2 the next day, he will not bother about it.

In most cases, day traders have a high margin for losses, so they will not be worried about losing a few hundred dollars a day.

They will also set themselves high margins, which will counteract the losses. It is obvious that the ratio between the two will have to differ by a large margin, especially if the investor wishes to remain with hefty profits.

As you already know, penny stock traders try to earn a big profit by combining several small profits that they earn all through the day. A penny stock day trader will only be able to make a big profit if he selects 10 or 12 good stocks that will rise in value in the course of the day to leave him with a profit.

Not all day traders are penny stockholders, mind you, so it is not an exclusive feature of penny stock traders alone. There will be many other investors in the ring who will hold the same stocks for, possibly, a much longer time.

Why should you day trade in penny stocks?

Now coming to the main debate, why should penny stocks be traded on a daily basis? Well, there are many reasons for it and we will look at them in detail.

First off, as you already know, penny stocks are quite volatile and will keep moving up and down all through the day. A trader can earn a better profit if he holds the stocks for a single day than by holding them for several days. He will be wasting both his money and his effort, as the same stock will give him bigger profits if he buys it fresh every single day.

When you trade on a daily basis, you have the chance to know how much you are worth and don't have to wait another day to know your true worth. This is great for all those that wish to know exactly how much they have in their holding and plan their next investment.

A person considerably cuts down on the risk of an investment going bad by selling it off on the same day. The stock might never recover soon enough and you will be stuck with a headache that you will want to get rid of at the earliest opportunity.

Many companies that charge hefty brokerage fees for transactions generally double it when it comes to holding stocks for more than a day. They will make you pay a hefty sum for holding stocks of companies overnight.

It is also important to note that penny stock companies can wind up without a notice. They will be small companies making marginal profits and, if they deem it fit to wind up instead of continuing, your investment will be in danger. Even if they give you buffer time to sell stocks, if nobody buys them from you, your investment is sure to get stuck in a rut, so it is important for you to be well informed about the companies and not risk leaving behind an overnight investment.

These are some of the reasons why penny stocks are best traded within a single day. But it is surely not limited to just these. There can be many other reasons that make investors pick day trading as the best method to trade in penny stocks.

You can try out both day trading and holding techniques when it comes to penny stocks and use the one that works best for you. Remember that individual stocks require individual treatment and it would be wrong to generalize about anything.

Remember that you don't always have to day trade with penny stocks and can trade normally as well. Many prefer to do day trading because they see it as an opportunity to capitalize on a stock's ability to move up and down within a limited period of time.

By now you should have a great foundational knowledge for trading with penny stocks. We've looked at the different types of stocks, how to predict their behavior, what to look for in analysis, and how to day trade. Now let's take a moment to look at some general dos and don'ts of penny stocks.

Chapter 17: Mistakes To Avoid

While it might be hard to internalize properly, no one trades with a 100 percent success rate with any degree of reliability. This doesn't mean that there aren't lessons to be learned from every failed trade, however, and it is important to look back on each after the fact and ensure that you stuck to your plan no matter what. As long as this is the case, then you have done right by the trade, even when it does not work out to the end. If you ever hope to truly trade successfully then it is important to separate the end result of a trade from your performance in said trade and analyze both separately to ensure the best results.

Choosing a broker at random: With so many things to consider, it is easy to understand why many new penny stock traders simply settle on the first broker that they find and go about their business from there. The fact of the matter is, however, that the broker you choose is going to be a huge part of your overall trading experience which means that the importance of choosing the right one should not be discounted if you are hoping for the best experience possible. This means that the first thing that you are going to want to do is to dig past the friendly exterior of their website and get to the meat and potatoes of what it is they truly offer. Remember, creating an eye-catching website is easy, filling it will legitimate information when you have ill intent is much more difficult.

First things first, this means looking into their history of customer service as a way of not only ensuring that they treat their customers in the right way, but also of checking to see that quality of service is where it needs to be as well. Remember, when you make a trade every second counts which means that if you need to contact your broker for help with a trade you need to know that you are going to be speaking with a person who can solve your problem as quickly as possible. The best way to ensure the customer service is up to snuff is to give them a call and see how long it takes for them to get back to you. If you wait more than a single business day, take your business elsewhere as if they are this disinterested in a new client, consider what the service is going to be like when they already have you right where they want you.

With that out the way, the next thing you will need to consider is the fees that the broker is going to charge in exchange for their services. There is very little regulation when it comes to these fees which means it is definitely going to pay to shop around. In addition to fees, it is important to consider any account minimums that are required as well as any fees having to do with withdrawing funds from the account. At the same time, be sure to keep any eye out for any additional benefits that might come with the account including things like free classes to enhance your skills.

Trying to make do with old technology: While taking your first steps into being a penny stock trader doesn't mean that you automatically need to go out and spend $2,000 or more on a new computer, it does mean that the technology you are using matters. As the most common way that penny stocks are traded is via day trading, it is important to consider what type of technology your competition is going to be using and then work to be in the same league, if not in the same ballpark.

This means you are going to want to have a computer that is up to the task as well as a video card that can handle at least two, if not three monitors. Additionally, you will want to have a backup internet connection just in case your primary connection goes down. While this might sound like an extravagance now, it will only take one use of it to complete a crucial trade which a given stock is in the money for it to pay for itself. Along these same lines, invest in a landline just in case everything goes down and the only recourse you have is to call your broker on the telephone. Remember, may penny stock trades are going to hinge on having split second timing, don't hamstring yourself by making do with a single laptop from the start of the decade, sometimes you really do need to spend money in order to make money.

Choose the wrong moment to get in on the action: During the early days of your trading career it is perfectly natural to feel overwhelmed from time to time which means that when you see an ongoing trend it can seem like a good idea to jump on it now and then ask questions about the specifics once the smoke clears. While you are sure to get lucky from time to time, the fact of the matter is that trends are only as good as the patterns they are a part of. Remember, the earlier that you get in on an emerging trend the more likely you are to profit from the movement that it generates. As such, if you spot a trend that is just about to peak, it is better to do your research and wait to get in on the next round of the cycle rather than jumping in at a point where you put yourself at risk for a loss, especially when you have no data with which to infer when it is coming.

Failing to balance research with what is going on in front of them: Research is an important part of a successful career trading any stocks, and penny stocks in particular. This doesn't mean that it is the end all and be all when it comes to making good trading decisions, however, as it is important that you always take your historical data with a grain of salt when compared with the current state of things. Remember, public sentiment is oftentimes just as important, if not even more so that what the research tells you and one of the things that separates novice traders from the experts is their ability to blend their research with the current state of things in order to determine where the two intersect at the current point in time.

On the other hand, traders who lean too heavily on public opinion while not taking the historical data into account can often make the right decision in the moment without then knowing how to back it up with the correct next step moving forward. Not taking the time to know if the current price is above or below the historical average means taking a risk on everything from potential profits to potential losses and is likely to work out just as poorly, if not even worse, than waiting around and doing nothing.

Not getting serious: When it comes to ensuring that you find success while trading penny stocks it is important to treat the entire experience like a job from the very first trade that you make. Remember, you are not just competing against the market as whole, you are competing against every other penny stock trader out there which means if you hope to more than throw your money away on fly by night companies you are going to need to get serious. What this means is trading at the same time each and every day, and committing to be up and at it each morning before the market opens doing your research to ensure you are not going in blind.

Furthermore, if you are treating penny stock trading like a job then this means you are going to be your own boss. This, in turn, means that you are going to need to look down deep inside yourself and find the strength and dedication to do the hard thing and dedicate yourself to the success you hope to find. More specifically, this means that in most cases when you have an active trade on the table you are going to want to glue yourself to the screen and not blink for even a second. The fact that you are sitting in your home staring at numbers on a screen that correspond to companies you have never heard of can easily start to make the entire experience feel surreal. This feeling will quickly dissipate, however, the second that you go to make yourself a sandwich only to find out that your current sure thing trade suddenly dropped out of the money while you weren't looking. Do yourself a favor and treat trading like a job and it will, in turn, reward you as if it was one.

Chapter 18: Methods Used To Predict Trading

Here is looking at some of the prediction methods that you can employ to predict the trends that stocks will follow.

Following trend

The first technique is known as trend following. This method is what most experts make use of to predict the fate of a stock. The general belief with which they operate is that the stocks that are rising will continue to rise and those that are falling will continue to fall. Using this method makes it very easy for them to invest in stocks. Not to say this technique will always work. But it will in most cases and so, it is a good technique to adopt.

Contrarian trading

Contrarian trading is what many experts use in order to avail lasting profits in the stock market. The contrarian way of thinking is the opposite of trend following. They will invest in stocks that are falling and sell the ones that are rising. The investor believes that the falling stocks will start to rise and the rising ones will start to fall. This type of thinking is a great way to judge stocks. You have to remember that it will work for you only if you know to pick the best stocks.

Candlesticks

Candlesticks are a statistical method of predicting stock trends. You have to place candlesticks on the graphs with a certain pattern in mind. You have to look at the highest point and then the lowest point that the stock has reached. Then you have to find the middle path and identify the levels that the stock prices will reach. Since this is a statistical method you have to do a few calculations for it. If you are not adept at it then you can avail the help of a friend.

Price action trading

Price action trading is another classic method that investors use to predict the trend of stocks. As investors it is extremely important to know how the prices will rise and fall. For this, they will look at the stocks monthly trends and predict which ones will rise and which ones will fall. Say a stock rises on the first of a month and then falls mid-month. The trader will be prepared for this and wait till mid-month to buy the stocks and then sell it during the first week of the next month to remain with a profit. You have to identify and follow a similar trend.

Range trading

Range trading refers to trading within a range that is pre-determined by the trader. So he or she will know what the upper limit is and what the lower limit is. He or she will trade within that range. Say the upper limit is $50 and the lower limit is $5. Within this range, the trader will buy and sell the stocks. They will not bother if the price goes lower than $5 or higher than $50. They are only bothered about the price staying in the same range.

Rebate trading

Rebate trading is a great option for those that are just starting out with stock trading. It is a technique where ECN's are used to trade. In an ECN, you make an investment and pay a commission towards it. The system will invest your money in the market. There will be many investors like you who will individually pay the commission and the company will profit from it. This is seen as a safe method to employ, as the ECN will do a good job at creating a large market and have enough money pooled in to invest in the best companies.

News following

News following refers to watching the news and looking for stock trends. As an investor, it will be important for you to keep tab of all the stocks' news and see which ones are doing well and investing where will help you remain with a profit.

You have to read about the company reports and see if any mergers or acquisitions have occurred in the recent past. You should also check for any products that were launched of late. All these will positively impact the price per stock and investing in them will reward you.

Swing trade

Swing trading is a good technique to apply to trade in stocks. It is a technique that you apply after you successfully identify the trend of a stock. Now suppose you bought a stock at $2. It fell to $1.5 and you decided to sell your stocks. You will then have to buy the stock at the same price point where you decided to vacate your position. Then, you wait until the price reaches $3 or $5 and then sell it for a profit. This technique will help you remain in profit.

Artificial intelligence

Artificial intelligence is a technique where you allow the computer to do all the calculations for you. You have to feed in data into it and allow the computer to give you the results. The computer software will do all the calculations for you and tell you which the best stocks are to invest in. It will get it right about 90% of the time but that 10% will always remain elusive. You have to try and use a combination of candlesticks and this method in order to see positive and sustainable results.

These form the different prediction methods that you can use to predict a stock's trends.

Chapter 19: The Difference In Penny Stock Trading. In The Us, Canada And Uk.

AMERICAN PENNY STOCK

Penny stock is also known as micro cap equity in the United States of America. There is no clear or generally accepted definition for the this term. Some defines them as a share in a company which trades for less than $5 or those which trades for pennies, while others define them as a company trading off on major market exchanges such as American Stock Exchange. They are usually traded on more obscure market such as the Pink Sheets. These definitions often cause contradictions. For example, there are very large companies, based on market capitalizations, that trade their stocks below $5 and there are also very small companies that trade their stocks above $5 per share. Furthermore, there are also very large companies trading in pink sheets which trade their stocks for more than $5 per share.

Advantages and disadvantages.

Traders who are speculative are engrossed in investing to micro cap equities because of several advantages. Amongst these advantages are: they are highly volatile, they can make large movements in prices over a short period of time, and it requires less capital as initial investment.

On the other hand, the more old-fashioned investors stay out from investing in micro cap equities because of several reasons. One of these reasons is that the fundamental companies are often not secure. Second, many shares are too unstable in terms of price and on percentage basis. Lastly, these companies don't pay dividends.

Investing in penny stocks.

These are by nature highly speculative. Investors of these stocks have to trade quickly. Investors have to be updated with what is going on with the stocks as these can make or lose money in a span of hours or even minutes. An investor should be quick in deciding what to do with them, whether to sell or keep it to avoid losing large amount of investment.

If one is planning to investing them, a review on popular stock message boards and various stocks related newsletters will be helpful in deciding which is best as of the moment. To be an effective investor, one must be well knowledgeable with the history of the performance of these stocks.

CANADIAN PENNY STOCK

Canadian penny stocks open a lot of doors to potentially successful small Canadian companies before they become recognized for their capabilities to construct shareholder value. A Canadian stock is considered as a share that trades below $5. They can be bought through the TSX Venture Exchange and the Toronto Stock Exchange. Those in Canada focus on technology and commodities. Canada's economy is booming and many individuals are buying stocks from that country due to their quality universities and graduates as well as abundance of natural resources.

For you to purchase Canadian penny stocks, you will have to go to a stockbroker that can buy Canadian stocks. All Canadian stock trades are established in Canadian dollars. As with any hot penny stock, you'd want a company that is heading towards a positive direction, developing competitive products and increasing their sales.

If you are a US investor, you basically have 3 choices. First, you can purchase pink sheets. Secondly, you can open an account with a Canadian broker. And Thirdly, you can open an account with a US broker that has entry to Canadian securities. With pink sheets, you get a listing of companies that are available every day. If you are going for this, do as much research as you can by reading newsletters and talking to people for instance, since this is an unregulated secondary market. As with the remaining choices, the companies are often listed on the TSX Venture Exchange until they satisfy the requirements for listing of the Toronto Stock Exchange. Moreover, the broker might be able to offer extra research services. When it comes to the first and third choices you stay away from the cost of currency exchange while purchasing and selling.

Here are the basic steps to buying Canadian stocks:

First, let your broker know you are interested in buying Canadian penny stocks. The broker then purchase these stocks through the Toronto Stock Exchange. Consult with your stock broker regarding what stocks are steady and going up. These will be the stocks in which you want to invest. Avoid investing in a company whose records show instability. Then, it's time to invest in the amount of money you want in the penny stock you picked. With stock trading and investment, you can gain much more for your money compared to conventional stocks and the rewards can be just as profitable. Your next step would be to visit the Toronto Stock Exchange website everyday or as often as you can to be updated. Observe how your stocks grow and expand in the Canadian economy.

Some of the advantages of penny stock trading in the UK include:

1. No Minimum Capital Requirement: Who would not be attracted to a no minimum capital requirement when it comes to making an investment? As money is tight nowadays, investment opportunities requiring only no minimum capital will be popular and more people will be interested in them. It is rare that investment opportunities requiring only a few hundred dollars come along,

thus with penny trading, people can invest a humble amount and still earn a good return.

2. Higher Earning Potential: In trading, the potential to earn is always high just as long as you have the necessary skill. The low

investment amount ($500 or less) needed to engage in penny stock trading just made trading even more accessible to investors who can only afford to put in a little amount of investment.

3. Stock Dividend Potential: Some penny stocks offer stock dividends, which will increase your total amount of shares without actually buying more shares.

4. Minimum Loss: Investing in trading always poses a great risk of loss. However with penny stock trading, investors would still be able to stand up again and invest after a loss since the risk amount that could probably be lost will only be a small portion of their funds. This is done by using sound money

management.

Investing money in trading is much like investing in any other business or money-making venture. There is always a risk of going bankrupt or losing the investment and this is part of the whole business venture.

For people wanting to try out stock trading without a large sum of money to start with, penny or micro capital stock trading are a good start. Trading in very small amounts may not yield that fast or that much return of investment but it is a good start. The important thing is to take advantage of opportunities that come along. Considering the advantages that an investor can have in penny stock or micro cap trading, it will not be for long before many more people take advantage of this opportunity as well.

Chapter 20: The Secrets To Making Profit

Penny stock trading is undoubtedly high risk, which gives it the benefit of being high profit as well. However, you will not make a profit without a few essential tips to help you along. If you are used to trading normal stocks and bonds, you will find that the strategies you employ in those markets, will not give you the best results with penny stocks. You need a new set of skills. You need to change your perspective towards making profit. Here is what you should look for.

Financials

This has been mentioned in research, though it is so crucial that it is worth emphasising so that it remains top of mind for any potential penny stocks trader or investor. Before you would make any investment in a company, you would typically check to see their financial standing, as this will play a part in whether you get your desired return. The same applies when you are looking to invest in penny stocks. Find out about the financial statements for the company that you are looking to invest in and go through them in detail. They should be current, and if possible, you should look at the statements for the past three years so that you can identify any patterns. If the penny stock that you want to invest in is from a company that does not have financial statements, or those which are available are of questionable quality, then you should not invest in these stocks as you will not make a profit.

Underlying Business

This ties in to growth within a sector or an industry which will determine whether purchasing a specific penny stock is a good idea. As penny stocks are high risk and fraught with corruption, it is possible that you will come across a shell company. This is a company that simply exists on paper, and does not have any real business operations. When dealing with shell companies, you will notice a high volatility in the shares as they are pumped into the market to feed in to high demand from potential investors, and then they are dumped, bringing down the price substantially and leaving you at a loss. If you are keen on making a profit, you must find a company which is real with business operations that you are able to verify.

To get this information, you can check sites like Yahoo Finance and Google Finance as these will also include news about your chosen penny stock. If nothing comes up, then it is an indication that you are not choosing the right company. The OTCBB is also an excellent source of information for the penny stock market.

Play the Pump and Dump

The penny stocks that you are trading may be from a legitimate source, yet even then, the pump and dump strategy may be used by someone who is looking to make a profit. If you find yourself caught up in this scenario, you should not panic. Instead, you can strategize so that you create an excellent profit for yourself. They key to making a profit here is knowing when you should sell, by being able to identify the patterns in trading.

Profit Percentage Gain

Put a cap on the amount of profit that you are willing to get from each trade, and resist the urge to get greedy. Greed is the reason that many penny stock traders make massive losses, as they want to keep pushing their returns in the hope that they will gain more. When you are on the rise, the moment that the trade reaches the profit percentage gain that you had established for yourself, you should pull out., This gives you the room to decide whether you want to re-invest in that penny stock or move on to a different option.

Turnaround Companies

These are companies that have gone through bankruptcy and are now coming up again. They may be going through a period of restructuring and have the backing of excellent investors. This means that during the restructuring process, the shares that they sell will be cheap, qualifying as penny stocks. Nonetheless, they are only moving in one direction and that is up, therefore as they increase in their success, the value of their stock is also expected to go up. This means that you will make a sure profit.

Pay Attention

If you want to consistently make profit, the main secret is that there is no short cut. You need to commit your time and energy to the process. One way is to always pay attention. This calls for you to pay attention to what is happening with the price of your stock, possibly taking an entire day to evaluate its movement. Doing this will make it easier for you to determine the patterns of increase and decrease in value that it has. This will make it easier for you to know when you should buy or sell.

While you are paying attention, do not lose sight of what penny stocks really are. These are short term investments and they are not suited to changing your financial future. This is because they are speculative in nature. If you make the right decisions through well thought out strategies, great – you make a profit. They should make up only a small section of your portfolio and should not be your entire portfolio.

Chapter 21: Trading Penny Stocks

High risk investments are a preference of many stock traders because of the expected high returns if things work out well as per your plan. Investing in penny stocks entails investing in stocks of small businesses that have a high potential for growth. There is usually no guarantee that these businesses will do well in the market but in the event that they do, the investor stands to benefit a lot from it. Penny stocks are highly risky because such small companies can collapse any minute and this means that you could lose all the money that you have invested in it.

Trading in penny stocks is therefore a serious affair that need to be well thought of before one puts their money into the investment. If you have already studied them well and you have made up your mind, it is time to start trading.

Develop your trading strategy

Success in stock trading is mainly determined by the stock trading strategy one uses and this is not exceptional for penny stock trading. You need a penny stock investing strategy that you will stick to the end in order to meet all your trading goals in the end. You have to always be prepared to face risks in this kind of trade. Many penny stocks have been branded unworthy of investing by expert traders, therefore you should know from the beginning what you are up against. The fact of the matter is that only a small percentage of all penny stocks can guarantee a good return for investors.

The kind of strategy that you will use in trading will be determined by a number of factors:

Your investing needs

Due to their high risks, penny stocks are not suitable for long term investors. If you have long term savings plans, it will not be advisable to invest in such kinds of stocks. The risk of loss is quite high and if you are saving for the future then you could end up losing so much money in a matter of minutes. If you have short term investment needs on the other hand, you will do so well in penny stock investing. Such kinds of stocks are good for investors who prefer to buy and sell frequently.

Your constraints

There are certain constraints that are really hard to negotiate and investors must consider them as well in determining the way that they will trade in penny stocks. If for instance there are certain stocks of a certain company that you cannot invest in, you need to choose a trading strategy that will not compromise on that. Some investors or traders have inherited some stocks as well and they will not let those go for personal reasons. You need to be aware of all this so as to know where to start trading.

Your risk tolerance

Just like in all the other kinds of stocks, there are penny stocks that are more risky than the others. There are those stocks that have high trading volumes and this makes them better than those that have low trading volumes. You have to be wise in your choice. In order to balance the amount of risk that you can take with the kind of returns that you are expecting. Ask yourself how far you are willing to go just so that you can get the kind of returns that you are eying from that investment. This should guide you on the kind of strategy you should trade with.

Your return expectations

Every investor has some kind of expectation on every investment that they make. The kind of return that you are expecting from your stocks portfolio will guide you to the kind of strategy that is right for you. People differ so much in what they require from their investments, that is why there are different strategies for different penny stocks investors. The kind of returns you want will also tell you how aggressive your trading strategies should be, because you have to meet your requirements in the end.

Always be ready for a loss

Penny stocks are very cheap when compared to the high value securities and the main reason why this is so is because there is always a high risk for loss. Many companies eventually fail and investors lose so much of their investments. Investors should always be aware of this so that in case it happens, they will not be affected so much. That is why it is good to diversify when you are investing in such stocks. Some businesses succeed in the end and this means that you can enjoy some good returns after all, but always be prepared for the worst to happen so that you will accept the outcome and move on with ease.

Purchasing Penny Stocks

Once you know the companies that you are going to invest in and you have your trading strategy well developed, it is time to make your first purchase. You will need an investment account for this. Register with a trading platform so that you can start making trades right away. You have to ensure that you are registering in a trading platform that will give you access to penny stocks though, since there are those that do not allow penny stock trading.

Beginners in stock trading will have to start here. Create an account and deposit some money into your account that will be used for your first penny stocks purchases. Cofounder the commission charges at all times, because there are trading platforms that will charge more than the others. You also need to consider your trading needs as well when choosing the right trading platform.

Traders who already have trading accounts for other stocks can use the same account to buy their penny stocks. You just have to check out the kind of plan you have signed for to see the kinds of charges you will face once you start trading in penny stocks.

Monitoring your investments

The value of penny stocks changes rapidly, so an investor has to be on the lookout at all times in order not to miss a chance to buy or sell their stocks. You need to monitor all the stocks that you have invested in closely at all times to know when to make a move. Always buy when the prices are low and sell immediately the prices go up so as not to miss the chance to sell at a profit.

You also need to keep a close eye on your portfolio's performance to know how well or even how badly you are doing every so often. This will motivate you to work harder especially if you are not doing so well already.

One thing that investors need to know is that they should maintain the same trading strategy throughout. Your trading strategy has been well developed, with great considerations, therefore changing it in the middle of trading just because you are not getting the expected returns is a bad idea. You have to be consistent in stock trading if you want to be a successful trader.

Keep investing. Penny stocks are not fully reliable; therefore, an investor should be ready to keep investing in order to enjoy some profits from them. Sometimes you will realize that some stocks are not doing so well and the only option you have at that point is to sell the off then buy those that you feel are doing better. Once you start trading, you will be able to see what is happening in the stock market clearly to be able to get serious in trading for the small profits.

Conclusion

We have come to the end of the book. Thank you for reading and congratulations for reading until the end.

I truly hope you found the book valuable and actionable enough to walk you through your penny stocks investment journey. Use the information you've learned here to get started while setting yourself up for success from the onset.

Thank you and good luck!